PENGUIN
SPECIALS

Penguin Specials fill a gap. Written by some of today's most exciting and insightful writers, they are short enough to be read in a single sitting – when you're stuck on a train; in your lunch hour; between dinner and bedtime. Specials can provide a thought-provoking opinion, a primer to bring you up to date, or a striking piece of fiction. They are concise, original and affordable.

To browse digital and print Penguin Specials titles, please refer to **www.penguin.com.au/penguinspecials**

ALSO BY XU XI

Dear
Hong Kong

An Elegy For A City

XU XI

許素細

PENGUIN BOOKS

UK | USA | Canada | Ireland | Australia
India | New Zealand | South Africa | China

Penguin Books is part of the Penguin Random House group of companies
whose addresses can be found at global.penguinrandomhouse.com

Penguin
Random House
PENGUIN BOOKS

First published by Penguin Group (Australia) 2017

1 3 5 7 9 10 8 6 4 2

Cover design by Di Suo © Penguin Group (Australia)
Cover photograph by Yang Wang © Penguin Group (Australia)
Text design by Steffan Leyshon-Jones © Penguin Group (Australia)
Printed and bound in Hong Kong by Printing Express

Grateful acknowledgement is made for permission to reprint extracts from the
following works: *The Waste Land* by T.S. Eliot by permission of Faber and Faber
Ltd; *City at the End of Time: Poems by Leung Ping-Kwan* 形象香港: 梁秉鈞詩選,
Edited and Introduced by Esther M. K. Cheung; translated by Gordon T. Osing
and Leung Ping-kwan, by permission of Hong Kong University Press.

penguin.com.au

ISBN: 9780734399380

FSC
www.fsc.org
MIX
Paper from
responsible sources
FSC™ C012285

CONTENTS

For Mum & Dad with all my love
and in memory of my brother
Felix Goebel-Komala
who left us way too soon

In the Time Before

In this time before the *yet-to-come,* that Chinese future tense 未來 or 將來, the future moment in question being the year 2046, I have already begun saying goodbye to my city. See, see, I still call Hong Kong 'my' city, the way Xi Xi once did, this other Hong Kong writer whose pen name tracks closely to my own byline, except that unlike me she writes in Chinese. I have been occasionally complimented for her work, or been contacted about her books, such as her novel *My City,* the one that of course I did not write. Hers was a stunning work, something that spoke so well to me of a vision of this city when I was still the fledgling scribe trying to put my HK into words. See, see, my city has already become 'my HK', an abbreviation dating back to my birth and childhood

1

here, a residency that carried through to adulthood in a spasmodic fashion. Almost everyone uses initials, followed by a surname, when their Cantonese name is turned upside down into English. There are probably hundreds of HK Wongs, Chans, Lees, Maks, Leungs, *et al,* and a number are undoubtedly men. 'H' could be the Cantonese 學 or *hok,* meaning to study, a good character choice for a name in my education-obsessed city. As for 'K', take your pick, as so many characters with a 'K' sound denote something masculine, making these all suitable choices for a boy's name in Cantonese. If I seem a little repetitive about 'Cantonese' rather than 'Chinese', it is because this southern dialect[1] is the real language of my HK, much more so than the two other official ones, English and *Putonghua*[2].

So my voice is not a *vox pop,* this English-language story I tell, this attempt at remembering my version of the city as a local foreigner. I am a native daughter, born and bred here, a child of 'overseas Chinese' *wah kiu* migrants from Indonesia, who happens to be an English-language writer of fiction and who is, for a

1   There are linguists who argue that Cantonese is in fact a language and not a dialect. Not being a linguist, I make no academic judgement but use the term 'language' as a matter of common sense about what ordinary people speak. Besides, Cantonese is termed one of the three official 'languages' of Hong Kong.

2   A transliterated Chinese term meaning common or ordinary language used to denote Mandarin Chinese, the official language of the People's Republic of China. English-language publishing does not like to use English-like words that its readers can't pronounce, so you often will see 'Mandarin' referred to as the language. This footnote is to satisfy nitpickers – of which there are many among readers of books about Hong Kong – who would take exception to use of the term 'Mandarin', since it can be considered politically incorrect. I sometimes use it if the context fits, since I believe language should not be unnecessarily convoluted without good cause.

change, trying to tell some of the facts of her life in a memoir, the way the genre demands.

What will happen after 2046, or, more accurately, 2047, the year when something is actually supposed to happen to HK? Once upon a time, we used to say: *What will happen after 1997?* That was the year of the great handover, when my HK returned like a prodigal child to his real parents, the nation of China, having spent too many adoptive years with his foreign parents, Britain. He was still a young man then, a boy really, just barely out of adolescence. This is the problem of belonging to families that are very, very old, ancient even, with not hundreds but thousands of years of history, because you remain a 'youth' for a long, long time. Some years after that first rite of passage, that handover-takeover moment (depending on whose version of history you read), I tried to interview HK about his history. He was a petulant interviewee, but got the facts right even though his perspective was biased in favour of himself.[3] That is the problem with 'history', written as it is by all who consider themselves winners, regardless of the facts.

But the problem at hand is 2046. Besides its notoriety as a dystopia fantasy sci-fi romance Hong Kong film by Wong Kar-wai, the only director who could successfully

3   This interview appeared in my one and only entirely nonfiction, mostly factual book, an essay collection *Evanescent Isles: From My City-Village* (Hong Kong University Press, 2008), which was badly typeset, inexcusably so, most likely with the bottom line in mind. This is the fate of a writer: publishers do with your writing what they will. However, you the reader should still buy the book and read the essay titled 'A Short History of Our Shores' if you would like a biased history of my city, as told to me by the city of Hong Kong.

produce a feature with all those adjectives under such a moniker that is *not* a 'political film', the year 2046 is in fact a highly political future moment, the way 1997 once was. It is a year that colours anything I write about my life in this city, and is a reason I am saying goodbye to my city in the 'Dear John' letter that follows in these pages, a 'Dear HK' prolonged goodbye. The year 2046 is when our current life will end. It's a 'will' construction rather than a 'might' construction because here is how our future reads in Article 5 of the Basic Law, the one that went into effect on 1 July 1997: *'The socialist system and policies shall not be practised in the Hong Kong Special Administrative Region, and the previous capitalist system and way of life shall remain unchanged for 50 years.'* Hence, 2046 is the last year before our known way of life ends on 30 June 2047 (check my math – I flunked math in my school leaving exam and am, after all, a fiction writer). Since I'm writing a memoir in the form of a Dear John letter to say goodbye to HK, mine's not to reason the whys and wherefores to interpret Article 5, which is best left to legal minds to debate and political minds of that future moment to enact. Instead, let me think about language – since that is the only tool a writer has – and the latter part of Article 5 that speaks to a fifty-year period of frozen time for an unchanged 'previous capitalist system and way of life'.

The trouble with a deep freeze is that you have no idea what will happen when you unfreeze, especially after such a prolonged time. As it is, you worry about defrosting the chicken that has sat in your freezer for a month or so, purchased with all good intentions to cook and consume before its use-by date, but somehow, chicken never quite appeals to my home-cooking taste buds when all the Chinese cuisines available in HK restaurants do a much better job than you can. Future tense is like that: desire suspended, more imaginary than real.

So HK, this love of my life (albeit an oftentimes tiresome and petulant lover) is in semi-suspended animation, with only his head sticking out of the deep freeze, so that he can continue to yell at me about how upset he is. Have you ever been in a relationship with a hopelessly maimed lover? Well, perhaps not maimed, since he willingly placed his otherwise functioning body into this frozen state, leaving only his head at work. All head but no heart does not a lover make (never mind the frozen corporal reality). Do you wonder that our relationship has become at least slightly maimed?

And so, Dear John, let me begin my goodbye. You will scream and rail, of that I have no doubt, but to mitigate your pain let me recall happier times, or at least past times, when we lived through our previous capitalist system and way of life. Let me recall for you some of what that life has been, was, and still is all about in this, our unchanged moment. Perhaps that will give you some comfort, this serenade to you, HK, oh city of my heart. *Quizás, quizás, quizás?*

I

Dear John, I mean, HK.

Dear HK, I had not planned on saying goodbye. Not yet. We were going to have many more years together, our love affair peaking and valley-ing as it has, as it does . . . oh, I knew I would leave you one day, when age caught up to my transnational life and it would no longer be possible to embrace such an immovably petulant, albeit persistent lover.

But now is too soon, when I am only in my early sixties, and when sixty, we hear, is the new forty. The grand departure was meant for the long run, although definitely before 2047, that defining date . . . that 未來將來 *yet-to-come* moment when two systems will somehow be compressed into one. When the mainland of China will actually take hold of your fragrant harbour, those waters between lands and worlds.

How do you write a Dear John letter to this most magical harbour in the world?

My father never did. In 1949, Dad flew into the city for the first time from Shanghai, having missed the flight that crashed, or so our family lore goes. He was studying at St. John's University, where he managed to complete perhaps a semester, perhaps a year (it's never been clear to us exactly how long he spent there, but we know he did have a blast and that he spent some of his time there in winter because he told us often about the icicles hanging outside his window, a sight that fascinated him, this boy from tropical Java). He remained in Hong Kong, carped a lot about the culture and its inhabitants, and died here, suddenly, one night at home of an aortic aneurysm, silencing his carping about the city's future decline. My father loved that harbour, though, magically echoed in The Platters' rendition of 'Harbor Lights' on an album he spun, and he fired my girlish imagination by naming other harbour cities, especially Rio de Janeiro and Buenos Aires, neither of which he ever got to see, both of which I still hope to one day see. He used to stand next to me on our top-floor veranda in Tsim Sha Tsui late at night, as we gazed at our harbour view in silence. Even as a child, I knew how privileged this view was, how special these late nights with Dad were. Those nights when stars were brightly visible, even the Milky Way, in our still-clear skies. Before he left us, my father was proud of his Chinese city, more marvellous, he said, than even New York or London, where his two eldest daughters lived. Used to live. New York, where I, his eldest, still live, except when I don't.

My mother will never get to say goodbye to all this. Mum saw the harbour in a dream long before she sailed into Hong Kong, or so she often told us, a little in awe of her own inexplicable mind. She came, she saw, she conquered her chosen home, a problematic new home where she spoke Cantonese atonally off key (being tone deaf), but managed somehow, forcing herself to be understood in her third language at the markets with hawkers of vegetables, meats, live poultry and seafood, while bargaining with shopkeepers, tailors, jewellers and watchmakers, or when imploring teachers at her children's local schools to forgive our many trespasses, those red marks in our Chinese subjects, the Chinese she could neither read nor speak well and couldn't teach us, unlike mathematics and English. Mum never willingly gave up, though; *You can do anything if you try hard enough* was the motto she lived by, sometimes to her detriment. My mother arrived alone in Hong Kong after the war that truncated her Singapore boarding school education, entombing her back home in a Central Javanese village under Japanese occupation. She arrived alone with little money but a grand dream to study medicine and become a doctor (she was accepted to the University of Hong Kong, but alas, never went). Alone and hopeful, but a little too old for dreams, she instead perse-vered and became a pharmacist, met Dad and became our Mum. Conquered as best she could. In 2017, at the age of 97, she conquers still, physically robust despite all odds – she fell and broke her hip a few years earlier but recuperated from the operation and remains in good health – even though her memory is long ago gone, gone, gone, this Alzheimer's mind that is far more inexplicable than the one of her youthful prescience.

My parents remained faithful lovers of this city, having abandoned both their villages in Central Java, the land of their birth. They sometimes contemplated straying – to Hawaii, Minnesota, home to Indonesia, Ohio – but in the end they remained, even while exhort-ing us – my three younger siblings and I – to pack our bags, leave the nest, go west, to live our lives out there, elsewhere, anywhere but here.

But I returned. Mostly because I had to, or felt I had to. HK issued his 愛國 call, the homeland's tug at the patriot's heart, the way China called all overseas Chinese to return prior to the Cultural Revolution, to show how much you 'love your country' in the Great Leap Forward, to rebuild it and resurrect it to glory. It is the nationalistic certitude that a Chinese is forever a Chinese, no matter how long she is exiled from home. HK issued a similar call – 愛城 – love your city, I suppose, because no other city can *possibly* compare, no other can be your 'city-village', the home village of Li Po's famous poem that every Chinese overseas recites to salve her homesickness.

So I returned, once, twice, thrice, each time to stay for several years, a conflict of emotions, because I was kicking and screaming all the way until exhausted if not tamed, a shrew through and through. Always complaining.

We've had a prolonged and tempestuous affair, this dream harbour and I. At some point we made a truce, when I conceded, *Okay you win, I'm sort of still in love with you. What say we make you my Second Husband Village?*[4]

No comment, he replied.

Can the male of the species be a concubine?

So this is the currently personal: I am held captive right now in my harbour city because my mother has not yet died. How's that for an inappropriate thought? But my life has never been about being appropriate, so there's no reason to start now. Meanwhile, things here have improved a little since my long ago nights of living dangerously in these streets. Young Chinese women can sit at a hotel bar and drink, without men to accompany them, either Chinese or Western. The bartenders will not

4   Second Wife Village is the name given to Shenzhen, just across the border from Hong Kong in the mainland, where Hong Kong men keep their mistresses-cum-concubines, the second or 'little wife'. If she's ambitious, a second wife will find a way to produce a son by her man, as this may allow her to unseat the first Hong Kong wife, the legal one.

whisper. The waitresses will not sneer, upholding some superior moral code. Security will not show them the door for moonlighting with intent. This at the bar of the very same hotel where you once told yourself, *Hold your head up, walk across the lobby and out the door into that early morning light by staring down security because* you *know you are not a whore, even if they don't.* No whispering gossip by other females who barely know you – *Oh that* one, *she* goes into bars unaccompanied, imagine! – whispers that flit back into your auditory range so that at twenty-something you told yourself, *Get the* hell *out of this tight-assed town and never, ever come back. Never.*

Can the male of the species be a concubine? Frankly, my dear, this is the political-personal-pragmatic dilemma that still worries my existence as I stroll down lovers' lane, arm in arm with this no-longer-fragrant harbour, this love of my life that insistently lingers, crooning *quizás, quizás, quizás,* like Osvaldo Farrés did in 1947.

In this time before the yet-to-come . . . of our tenuous, tenuous future, what stories do we tell ourselves? Let us begin here with once upon this time, at this moment of writing an epistolary heartbreak.

*

In 2017, we are delaying climax, holding back for a future which, we are certain, will turn out *more good,* as better articulates in Cantolish, our truest mother tongue, since it's rare to hear 'pure' Cantonese anymore, assuming we ever did, polluted as it has become by English, our former parent's tongue.

In 2017, our political landscape is littered with parties that divide and form new parties, even before the old ones have contributed substance to history. Not even we locals can distinguish between all the parties who shout about democracy and patriotism since the 'running dogs of Beijing' (unlike those of that other kennel) claim to represent both. Oh wait, that's not quite right, it was London we ran towards, wasn't it, yapping all the way? What must we anthropomorphise into now? Manic monkeys, whirling white snakes, prancing pangolins, dancing dolphins?

By 2015, we could barely keep track of the musical chairs or scandals in our last chief executive (CE) election – good wives, mistresses, unauthorised building works, a legality that a playboy of the east blithely ignores to construct his underground swimming pool until exposed by the still-free press. If, that is, an election by a chosen elite can indeed be called an 'election'. CY Leung, our current CE, is sanguine. Meanwhile, our former CE, Sir Donald Tsang Yam-kuen, has been convicted of corruption. (What, you mean an elected government official *shouldn't* accept favours from those who stand to profit from government contracts? Really, who knew.) During his tenure he traipsed around the world in bowties and splendour, confabbing with governments. (What, you mean we're *not* a city-state? Really, who knew.) In the end he sorely disappointed, this local Catholic boy who used to be *one of us,* a model public servant and son of a policeman, who should have known better. Really. Who would have known?

Oh dear John, you should be forgiven because politics was never your thing. You should stick to what you know and do best. Things like shopping, dining, sipping wine and dancing the night away in a *dolce vita* of sweet forgetting.

It's September, and all this political noise is something to ponder as we commemorate the one-year anniversary of Occupy.[5] Is the real problem the fact that we are not a nation-state, but forget this from time to time? Once upon a time in Hong Kong, 'national' meant 'foreign with Chinese characteristics'. Today we are Chinese with foreign characteristics, which translates into a troublesome lack of patriotism – at least according to Beijing.

When I'm flummoxed by the state of the city, I turn to statistics for solace.

5   Occupy Hong Kong, also known as the Umbrella Revolution, was a series of street pro-
     tests that virtually closed three districts in the city and lasted from 26 September to 15
     December 2014. Thousands of mostly young people camped in tents in the streets of
     Admiralty (as well as parts of Central) and Causeway Bay on Hong Kong Island, and
     Mongkok in Kowloon. The origin of the protest was a demand for universal suffrage in
     the election of the chief executive of Hong Kong, although it was clear from much of
     the signage and street art that erupted during the occupation that protestors were also
     concerned with other social and political issues, including the economic situation, a
     perceived erosion of long-established freedoms in the city and, in general, threats to the
     way of life that Hong Kong people have come to view as their right.

In 2015, a quarter of our working population exhibited signs of anxiety and depression, which is two and a half times the global average, or so the latest survey reports. Sixty per cent of respondents acknowledged that they were 'highly stressed due to their jobs'. Another recent survey tells us that 18 per cent of working persons need psychological treatment. Our work world does not have time for mental health; actually, Hong Kong grants limited space to psychology, this viral epidemic. *Unfair,* HK shrieks (sounding a little like the current CE), *stress is normal in urban life, and if properly managed will not interfere with being the happy percentage of those equations!* Mental health, we hear, is yet more propaganda from the West, that colonial past, a history we really must learn to forget.

There is always a 'latest survey' to measure the trouble we're in, this Western, socially scientific measure we willingly embrace, unlike psychology.

In 2015, the young and even the not-so-young dishonour Cantonese, silence Putonghua and remain in conflict with English. Our three official languages are in a sad state. During graduation at one public university, the languages of all official pronouncements were made only in English and Putonghua.[6] *No Cantonese?* I murmured. But my remarks went unheard. However, the names of the graduates were read either in Cantonese and Putonghua (surname first) or in English (last name last),

15

although almost all the Masters graduates of English sported what appeared to be Mainland Chinese names. Among the list of graduates, a few foreign names were accompanied by Chinese characters. The president and two deans intoned uncomfortably in non-native speaker English; the most liberated English speaker was the young graduate selected for the general address, a mainland student who, if we are to believe her, likes Hong Kong, learned a lot here and benefitted greatly from her global education opportunities through exchanges in Brazil and elsewhere. The national anthem was played instrumentally; we did not sing the Putonghua lyrics to 义勇军进行曲, although we did stand in silence, better behaved than fans at the World Cup qualifier football match, who booed[7] when it was played.

In this time before the *yet-to-come* D-Day of 2047, I wonder how many Hong Kongers will stand for the anthem, never mind learn and sing the lyrics? Will they be more or fewer than those in colonial times who

6   We dare not use 'Mandarin' these days, lest we be condemned as running dogs of the wrong master, even though much of the world is only just discovering that 'Putonghua' is in fact a word, never mind a language. Despite a 'globalised, superpower China', all this must still be glossed for comprehension by the global reader, meaning the English-language reader, the reader who is not yet entirely conversant with pinyin, the transliteration of choice for Chinese today – if you ask China. Then again, some diehard Sinophiles or Taiwanese might disagree, because in Taiwan and elsewhere, it still is possible to say Mandarin, coupled with Chinese, to mean a language.

7   Hong Kong fans have booed the Chinese national anthem at every match. FIFA investigated these anthem-booing incidents and censured and fined the HKFA 5000 Swiss Francs for the bad behaviour of local football fans. The November 2015 World Cup qualifier match between Hong Kong and China saw a separation of Hong Kong and mainland fans, each group consigned to different ends of the Mongkok stadium. The police deployed 1200 officers in Mongkok that day, the same number assigned a year earlier during Occupy in Mongkok, the district that experienced the most violence. One anthem, two nations? The November match ended in a draw.

refused to stand for 'God Save the Queen'? Back in the sixties, most of the local audience used to walk out of cinemas when the British anthem played after a film ended, a curious practice in entertainment patriotism that eventually ceased, but coloured my childhood. Why hasn't some scholar already conducted a survey?

In 2047, our fifty years as a Special Administrative Region is scheduled to end, along with our curious stature under China's 'one country, two systems' policy.

But as of this moment, writing in 2017, we are delaying climax because, frankly, we're exhausted by these never-ending trials of language, politics and social unrest. Who has time, never mind energy, for real love or commitment? If you don't like it here, leave. Isn't that the universal patriot's rant?

Should she go or should she stay? Frankly, my dear, HK doesn't give a damn.

Or does he?

In 2015, when I first started penning this Dear John letter, my HK is challenged by the controversy of the TSA. No, not the Transport Security Administration of the Department of Homeland Security that challenges air travellers to, from or within the US, but rather the Territory-wide Systems Assessment, a.k.a. the tests that local pupils and their parents dread, and that drive some youngsters to despair and suicide. Since 2011, tests are administered at Primary 3, Primary 6 and Standard (or Form) 3 to 'facilitate assessment learning by providing schools with objective data on students' performances in the three subjects of Chinese Language, English Language and Mathematics at the end of Key Stages 1–3'. these tests are compulsory for all government-sub-sidised schools. On paper, this sounds benign enough, but the reality is that schools endlessly, and some say mercilessly, drill the city's youngsters to achieve higher scores in order to raise their reputation and prestige. This pantheon of tests excludes the public exam for the HKDSE Diploma of Secondary Education, adminis-tered at Standard 6 to further distress youth.

Earlier in the year, the Hong Kong Professional Teachers' Union conducted a survey which reported that the TSA affected many teachers' daily workloads, requiring them to hold after-school classes as well as give students extra work in the form of practice tests. In June, some 70 per cent of primary school teachers called for the tests to be banned. In October, 30 000 Facebook users signed up for an event calling for the abolition of the TSA. By November, the debate was still raging.

In December, the city is abuzz with the Education Bureau's proclamation letter to schools that they must stop drilling students for the TSA, since these tests are not meant to be studied for, but are simply an assessment of the level of learning achieved. Schools that do not obey this directive might, they were told, receive a 'written warning'. The education minister then attempted to soothe ruffled feathers by telling schools to end drilling so that children could have a happy, relaxed Christmas holiday.

Meanwhile, Christmas has come and gone. School principals are furious, parents are furious, and the minister is once again apologetic for our tenuous education policies and practices. Talk show hosts on radio and TV chatter away with experts on all sides of this latest issue.

It is at times like these, when life proves overwhelmingly absurd, that memory speaks.

(1)

Memory speaks, and I am transported back to my upbringing here as a student of the local education system where I tried to be, but never was, that straight A student. A British colonial education that mirrored but did not exactly replicate the curriculum in the UK for all the government schools, which the majority of local students attended, including myself. What is memory, after all, if not a fiction to replay and revise the stories of our lives when the city becomes unmanageable? Unbearable, intolerable, irascibly impossible. What is memory, after all, if not a palliative to time, allowing me to ignore the sight of my HK disappearing before my very eyes?

However, some of my HK life *should* disappear. Eleven report cards, for instance, one to mark the end of each academic year at Maryknoll Convent School. Eleven years spent at that government-subsidised elite girls' school, begun in Primary 1 and ended after Form 5, meant that I had to take the SSEE (Secondary School Entrance Examination) in Primary 6 and the HKCEE (Hong Kong Certificate of Education Examination) in Form 5, two dreaded D-Day epochs that plagued my school life. What these report cards prove is that red marks persist until you eventually wake up and recognise that the cosine of anything does not teach you how to live. Algebra was a mental challenge, calculus a failed curiosity, but trigonometry! Trigonometry was entirely incomprehensible even though the equations were solvable. That thin, four-figure table reference volume with its microscopic columns of figures, one I clutched between its blue covers through secondary school, and which was eventually consigned to the library of oblivion. The whole bundle of report cards was wrapped in a greenish-brown paper, tied up with string and burnt. This 'chicken skin paper'[8] wrapping was once commonly used to cover textbooks for school.

All this remembrance makes me wonder why it's necessary, in our presumably more psychologically advanced times, to continue testing students even more frequently than before, when all that survive of those

---

8 雞皮紙, which just goes to show that food is never far from life in HK. The phrase conjures deep-fried chicken skin, a local delicacy that is, of course, exceedingly bad for you, which is why I still love it, despite twenty-first century health awareness.

years for me are some short letters to the city (which appear below), the true measure of this girl's education, far outstripping anything she memorised for all those exams, exams that made her question her very existence, wondering whether she too would have to make that suicide leap – *oh glorious martyrdom* – if her exam results did not blaze a sufficiently glorious future.

After the dreaded HKCEE examined me through my school's compulsory nine subjects – I failed two (Religion and Calculus), barely passed five (the three Sciences, Mathematics and History) and distinguished myself in two to no notice by anyone (French and English) – I left this elite girls' playground and parked myself for Lower Form 6 at a private co-ed school until fate intervened a year later.[9] I independently took the SAT, or Scholastic Aptitude Test, and did a few practice tests myself (so different from the years of tortured tutoring, cramming and mock exams that led up to the HKCEE). My SAT scores were fortunately noticed by universities in America, so I was able to avoid the suicide leap.

Lower 6 proved a glorious school year, and my most educational one. I paid no attention in class, played hooky frequently to indulge in *yum cha* at Red Ruby

9   My essay 'Et Tu Mon Père', published in that earlier book, *Evanescent Isles* (Hong Kong University Press, 2008), details the history of this episode of secondary school, during which I studied the sciences, even though I was originally streamed into arts, as befits my natural abilities.

Restaurant with my friends, and, at the end of the year, skipped all the final exams.[10] That report card most certainly did not survive. That year, I read and wrote as much as I wanted, and first began to understand that this writing thing I cared about more than school could maybe, just maybe, one day become my life.

*

The letters reproduced below were hidden under a large stone along the pathway of Maryknoll Convent School, the one below the primary section's covered playground. The cool earth preserved these scraps of lined paper, torn from blue-covered notebooks, on which these notes to the city were scribbled. The violet ink has faded. The school itself is a heritage site occupying the corner of Waterloo Road and Boundary Street in Kowloon; it was established by a liberal order of American Catholic nuns whose global mission is education and service to the poor. It was rumoured (because we schoolgirls thrive on gossip, the gothic and safely sexualised longings and desires) that, during the Japanese occupation, the fingers of nuns

---

10 I mean no disrespect to the private school in question. Although I was hardly a model student, I remain grateful to New Method College in Kowloon for providing me a year-long parking space so that I could legitimately complete six years of high school, a prerequisite for entry into American universities. I am grateful for their location, above 紅寶石, the excellent Cantonese restaurant that served daily dim sum to errant schoolgirls and boys, as I also am grateful for their co-ed enrolment, tired as I was of being surrounded only by girls. But what I am most grateful to that institution for is their winter school uniform, which included a tie and, as a result, taught me to correctly and swiftly tie a double knot, the Windsor, a memorable contribution to my life's education and a useful skill around future lovers and husbands.

23

cut off by soldiers were buried under those stones. The
letters, as if shaped by such mytho-logic, resemble notes or
memos, short if not always sweet.

My Secret Letters to HK

to	*him*
from	*me*
date	*aged 5 and a half*

I can't come out to play. Miss Yeung the tutor is here today. Mummy makes me study extra Chinese. I can't come out to play.

to	*him*
from	*her*
date	*aged 7*

Nyannh, nyannh, nyannh, nyannh, nyannh,
I'm better than you are
'Cos I'm a girl
And you're not.
AND you're a scaredy-cat
Boo!

(Mummy says I shouldn't shoot my water pistol at you any more because it isn't a nice thing for girls to do to boys.)

to	him
from	her
date	aged 9 and a half

You watch me at ballet school through binoculars from your bedroom. I do lousy cartwheels. What's so interesting about girls' underpants? You're silly. Why did you tell me this anyway? (Mummy says you're stuck up because your father's a doctor.)

to	him
from	her
date	aged 11 almost 12

Last night, you invited me to dance. All the other girls looked so grown up, while I looked like a child. I didn't even know what party dress to wear for my first dance so I wore my Girl Guide uniform instead, since we were invited by the Boy Scouts. My classmates are all older than me because I started school too early, and some of the older girls in our Guide company even wore heels and makeup. If I ever have a daughter I won't let her start school too young.

You felt sorry for me, I know, because I'd been sitting alone most of the night. It felt strange to slow dance with a boy. But I liked it.

So no, Virginia, there is no Santa any more or a

25

Sandman to bring you your dreams,[11] but it'll be okay because some things are going to change. Are changing. Will change. Have to change.

to	*him*
from	*her*
date	*aged 13*

Talking is even better than dancing. We agreed about that.

to	*him*
from	*her*
date	*aged 13 and a half*

Your letters make me happy. Did you know *Pamela* was the first epistolary novel? Mrs Liao, my English literature teacher, said so. I read it over the summer. It's a big book, rather dull, but in the end I found it sad. Pamela was pretty stupid. I don't want to have children, ever, especially not a girl. Do you?

to	*him*
from	*her*
date	*aged 13, almost 14*

11 Although The Chordettes, who recorded the song 'Mr. Sandman' in 1954, cannot compete with the likes of Taylor Swift or Adele today for global dominance, in 2015, one YouTube posting of the song still managed to attract over 16 million views before it was taken down. Which just goes to show that when it comes to what girls want from boys, nothing really ever changes and nostalgia is still as potent as it always was.

Mum doesn't like you. She denies it but in the same breath calls you *jaapjung*. Of all the local Cantonese attitudes she chose to adopt, why was this cruel prejudice the one she mastered best? I wanted to scream at her that she was wrong, wrong, wrong, but it's hard to do that, scream at your mother, I mean.

I'm *jaapjung* too, you know, although Mum would never call us that. It's just that neither of my parents are Caucasian, which makes me a different kind of 'mixed species'. Mum doesn't recognise that because she doesn't have any Indonesian blood, unlike Dad, or so she says. I don't believe her though because she's so much *less* Chinese than Dad, and her Chinese is lousy and she talks and behaves like an Indonesian. Dad reads and speaks Mandarin.

But You. I'm not sure what all this means for us so I'm writing this as a memo to my future self as a reminder.

to	him
from	her
date	aged 14

I wrote you a 'Dear John' letter but that was a lie, an untruth Mum told me to write. Made me write. I just didn't know how to say that one true thing because there are no words for feelings like this. She made me feel like a wicked child again, the one who screamed too much and ended up in hospital, needing to have her tonsils out. At least that's what she said at the time, terrifying me with my wickedness. I was five.

At the end of it all – her lecture, her 'mother knows best', her misreading of everything you and I are – she might as well have patted me on the head and said 'good girl' because that's what the whole thing felt like. She *hounded* me until I gave in. She's good at that (just ask my brother, he knows how she hounds).

But I actually feel sorry for Mum. Dad's broke, so she's always worried about money for our school fees, books and clothes, and at home we pretend like everything's okay. Dad doesn't talk much to me, or anyone, any more. What we do talk about when we talk about life is my future at university abroad, but I wonder, all the time, how will we afford it? You don't have to worry about that, do you? You live in an expensive home (Mum pointed that out about you too, when she saw the return address on your letters) and you have an English surname. I think that's why Mum doesn't like you, because she hates anyone who might be better off than us, because she thinks they'll look down on us if they knew the truth of our circumstances.

Better is relative, I told her once, and she glared at me as if I'd sworn at her. Sometimes, I do swear. They're just words after all, and why should we ever be afraid of language? I swear under my breath, usually when I sneak outdoors to the foot of the hill of the Royal Observatory to smoke (which she also doesn't know I do). Never to her face, though. I'd get in too much trouble.

You and I, if we ever meet again I'll tell you to your face that you were the first boy I ever loved, but I didn't have the guts to write that to you. More important, I'll tell you I'm sorry, so sorry for my lack of courage, my inability to commit a girl's first disobedience, even if an apology will never make up for my behaviour. I'll do this even though apologies are absurd. The point is to do the right thing in the first place.

You know, I would have telephoned but your mother doesn't like Chinese girls calling, even though she is Chinese. What you meant, I think, is that she doesn't want you going out with someone like me. You never had to tell me that. I knew when you said I couldn't ever call you at home, although I did look up your number in the phone book. I suppose that makes us even.

Funny how letters were okay.

Were better, more good.

The only thing I wish? That we had kissed at least once. French kissed, like in *The Thomas Crown Affair*. I adore Steve McQueen but movie stars are fiction. It would have been something to remember you by.

Goodbye.

to	them
from	her
date	aged sweet 16

So this is the Swan's solo flight, to be adored,worshipped, sent cards by three boys with crushes on you. How delicious that all three sent the exact same card (a want of imagination or a lack of consumer choice?). One boy was European, the second a kind of 'ABC', although not from a Western nation. And the third, who was that third, HK? I forget. Perhaps I never knew. I like to think he was a local Cantonese guy, because local Cantonese guys avoided me like cholera. Too dark-skinned, too outspoken, too forward. Not Chinese enough, not *authentic*. Authentic. Do you know how often girls at school said that to me, that I was not authentically Chinese? Which is why I preferred to hang out with the foreign and *jaapjung* girls. Surely in all those early years that made me so badly want to leave this city, there was at least one local guy who thought I could, like him, belong in Hong Kong? Or was I merely exotica, just another Suzie Wong?

II

Dear HK,
Shut up already.

In 2016, we are living in a city that is measurably at sea.
Our shoreline is unrecognisable to the cartographer of
fifty years ago thanks to the miracle of reclamation.
This city revels in man-made grandeur, such miracu-
lous engineering feats as HKG, an airport of the floating
world that connects our largest islands, and us, to the
world. Of all the shores in my sightline, however, it is
the coastal path along West Kowloon towards the New
Territories that obsesses me as 2017 dawns, this shoreline of the Rambler Channel. West Kowloon is close to
where I grew up in Tsim Sha Tsui, but it was rougher
then, and not the district for development, being more
water than land. Memory buoys bob, stranded between
liquid and solid, lost in this man-made geography as
if Earth must, *should,* constantly shift. Should I have

drowned earlier, thus sparing me this cockeyed rear view or 背景, as the past articulates in Chinese? Why obsess over an erased past, a lost waterway that borders the city's future arts district, assuming it ever gets completed.

In 2016, we end the year on the still unfulfilled promise of an arts district in West Kowloon. HK has been developing this plan *ad nauseam,* through international design competitions, via local arts experts in consultation with those from abroad, and has spent vast sums of public money on this enterprise. Further north along the Rambler Channel, HK closed the beaches for several years (including my beloved '19 ½ mile' one) due to excessively polluted water. It's been a long while since I've dared to swim in HK's surrounding seas. Once, back in the 1990s, I dove off a boat and emerged with an earache. A few times, less than half a dozen during the mid-to-late 2000s, I swam at the beach at Discovery Bay. But I stopped after my foot was entangled in some grotesquely man-made waste. The last time I entered HK waters was off Lamma Island in the early 2010s, at the beach furthest from the pier, on a hot day after hiking around the island with a friend from Taiwan. Mercifully, that last immersion was without incident.

*

But I was in the midst of contemplating my elegy to HK. How did I get distracted by this political parade beyond my window? *Note to self:* Do not write Dear John letters while gazing out windows, regardless of that romantic image. You should know by now that writing requires concentration, immersion in the dictionary, explorations of language in service of the genre. The reality of the task, not the fiction of the dream.

Back to the page we go.

> *Dear HK, of course you were the love of my life!*
>
> How often must I repeat myself? I came 'home' to stay three times (count them, three!) for long stretches, for at least seven years before I got the itch. Yes, you have been a constant lover, a generous one who never stinted when it came to money. But sweetheart, the Beatles said it well – *money can't buy me love.*
>
> And please, please, please, kindly shut up about 'corrupting foreign influences'.
>
> It's hard enough to tell you this but let's face it, we're older now and there's no need to mince words. I will leave you one day and yes it will be forever. Many other so-called Hong Kongers have done so who still think you're the best. So why should it matter if I am the detractor, the one who

offers a tad less adulation, a tad less idolatry or worship? At least I'm not singing about fifty ways to leave my lover, or embroiling you in a messy divorce. I will simply exit quietly one day, sneak out as it were, and never renew my HKID[12] again.

---

12 Acronym for the Hong Kong Identity Card, since this city likes its abbreviations that function like code. Besides, many Hong Kongers practice code-switching as a matter of language. Every foreigner teaching English as a second or foreign language in Hong Kong recognises this, regardless of their expertise or scholarship in the much touted academic discipline of linguistics, one that is heralded in the universities of Hong Kong and is a reason for maintaining 'English' as a discipline to be funded and taught. If China has her way, as she increasingly does in the running of HK, linguistics would exist only as a study of the Chinese language, which, in some local universities, is the reality, and English would no longer be the compulsory Medium of Instruction (or MOI) in publicly funded higher education. After all, the universities in China are able to graduate students who speak, read and write English as well as (and in some cases better than) many Hong Kong university graduates, and the MOI in China is most definitely not English. It is worth recalling, in this reflection on code and language, that one of China's most successful entrepreneurs, namely the founder of Alibaba, began his professional life as an English teacher. The reason that is of interest to me is: I am, after all, an English-language writer from HK, a being that should not exist, and certainly not thrive, since I am obviously a traitor to the language that should be mine. Fortunately, I became an American citizen, and the linguistic problem in the US is of quite a different stripe.

(2)

Echoes for this travelogue
through memory from:
'we travel with lots of stuff '
a poem by 也斯 Leung Ping-Kwan

The Rambler Channel flows along the western shore of the New Territories, separating Tsing Yi Island from the Kowloon Peninsula. As a girl, I used to eagerly anticipate trips to the '19 ½ mile' beach, where my family shared a shack with an Armenian-Portuguese couple and their only son, the dancer. He used to dance for us, this childstar of local films and performances, this talent too large for our city, this boy who, as a teenager, once spun for me Diana Ross's 'Ain't No Mountain High Enough' and who was obsessed by the music and movie of Woodstock. That was the year before I escaped to the US for the first time on a F-1 foreign student visa. When memory speaks, you tend to recall the way the world still somehow managed to open up for you, how the information river flowed towards you despite the constraints of your world.

But memory also relies on triggers. For me, the visual triggers are the home movies my father shot that my brother revived and preserved. My musical memory muscle is surprisingly robust, and I can recall songs almost at will to trigger memory. Would we remember if we could only rely on our brains, as they atrophy with age, as plaque hardens along the byways and pathways into a sea of forgetting? In my mother's Alzheimer's reality, even the triggers do not aid recall.

Back in the sixties, the waters were still moderately clean, the countryside rural and the city an affordable place to live. The city was poorer then, and the world did not beat a flight path to our shores. FILTH, they said, washed up because those who Failed in London Tried Hong Kong. The rest of global FILTH, in lesser numbers, also appeared: FINTH from New York, FIPTH of Paris, FIJTH from Johannesburg and the FISTH of Sydney. They were apparently all filth, 'white-skinned trash who joined our heap'. Our city was that faraway East and forgettable Orient, a transit stop for the world's FILTH, where the cheapest products were assembled for export, goods labelled 'Made

In Hong Kong', a tag implying lack of quality, a shameful moniker of capitalistic greed.

As a girl, I once visited a classmate who lived on the eighteenth floor of my building. In my then over-privileged existence, it was easy to believe that the whole world ate cake and sipped champagne to celebrate. The poor were the refugees from China who were lucky to have a future in my city, or so the more fortunate believed, wanted to believe. We did not need to feel too sorry for them because their lives could and would improve as long as they worked hard, obeyed British laws and bought into the promise of our East-West meeting point.

My Chinese classmate was not well off. The head of her household was a single mother; I never learned why her father was not around. She had invited me to visit, which I understood literally. It is only now, years later, that I realise her invitation in Cantonese – When you're free, come up and sit – was merely polite talk. There was no one to tell me[13] that this phrase was akin to the ubiquitous Cantonese expression 'have you eaten yet', which does not require a literal response. I was around

---

13 Elsewhere I have written that I had two mother tongues – ESL and CSL – English and Cantonese as second languages, since neither language was my parents' mother tongue. It took me years to feel that I had fully mastered English, a sorry admission for any author about the language of her writing, but there you are, you cannot change the truth or reinvent history, unlike nation states who do this willy nilly, in concert with the outlook of whichever government happens to be in power. To date, I still have not mastered Cantonese completely, and doubt I ever will. In HK, true bilinguals, never mind trilin-guals, with complete mastery of our three official languages, are few, especially among writers. Many bilingual or multilingual writers choose to write in one language at a time, since you never really completely master any language unless you are that rare linguistic genius, those born with that non-proverbial silver tongue in their mouth (opinion mine, with no corroboration I can cite as proof).

eight or nine and simply excited to discover a classmate who lived in my building.

It was in this anticipatory mood that I climbed the building's stairwell one flight to the eighteenth floor. The stairwell was dark and dank and smelly, a repository for each floor's refuse to sit overnight before being collected the next morning.

Here I must pause to describe buildings in HK. My apartment building was constructed in 1959 and was, at that time, the tallest in Kowloon. It was a great thrill to see it reproduced in my Chinese civics textbook, a rare moment for my sister and me, because the inclusion of our home made it a lesson of 社會 (literally, 'society', or the primary school subject Civics) that we could actually enjoy. The other Chinese-language subject we had to study was 國語 (literally, 'nation's language', which actually means literature), and both subjects were torture, given the discrepancy of the name of the subject vs. the actual content covered, as well as the rote memorisation required for mastery. Which is why I flunked out of Chinese after Primary 4, but that's another story. The real point is that my building officially only possessed seventeen floors. It is a truth universally known in HK that many buildings do not have a fourth floor due to the sound of the word 'four', which is a homonym for 'death'. The truth less universally known is that the top floors of many buildings are false levels. Some are

UBW,[14] such as the rooftop bedsit in which I currently reside atop my mother's flat. Others are the extra floor just before the rooftop that was perhaps not originally meant to house flats. To resolve this building dilemma, developers simply ensure that the lifts stop at the floor below, so that the so-called top floor, which is presumably part of the roof, can be developed as cheaper 'flats', to be sold as long as the government building inspector's silence can be bought. What can I say? This was before there was an ICAC, and ubiquitous requests for 'tea money'[15] required a literal response if you wanted life to be less than hellish. Which created, of course, its own kind of hell.

But I was on my way to the eighteenth floor. Until that day, I had not known anyone else lived up there. We lived in a penthouse flat that occupied both the seventeenth and eighteenth floors, and had an interior staircase down which all my siblings and I managed to slip-slide-tumble at least once; my brother's spill was

14 UBW, or Unauthorized Building Works, abound in HK residential buildings, including in the homes of the current CE and one of the contenders for the post in 2012 (the former removed it in compliance once this was reported in the media, while the latter's UBW hastened his downfall in the election). Which just goes to show that authorised building policies probably need to be addressed and perhaps re-imagined in the development of this vertical city.

15 The ICAC, or Independent Commission Against Corruption, was not established till 1974. Before that time things were accomplished through 'tea money', a bonus that the public paid to government servants under the British, which ensured the seamless execution of all those small and large tasks essential to daily urban life – collecting garbage, obtaining liquor licenses, dispensing with traffic fines, approving building plans, securing a gravesite or columbarium for a deceased loved one, procuring a place in an elite school for one's child, acquiring a license to operate a business and the like. Which is why the sight of young people waving British flags during protest marches or occupations irritate not only the Chinese government but also a lot of us older Hong Kongers, who recall that life was not always a bowl of lychees back in the 'good old days'.

memorably dramatic as he was playing Batman at the time and ended up crashing through the screen at the base of the stairs. My classmate lived in something less than a full-size flat, because it looked like a one-room space where she, her mother and younger sister lived and worked. Their work gave me pause. I had never seen any other child my age work in their home. Piles of plastic flowers, which all three of them would assemble, filled the space. This kind of take-home piecework was commonplace in the fifties and sixties, especially for residents of slums and public housing. But this was a private residence. I was served tea, and my classmate chatted with me about her life, all the while pulling one freshly laundered handkerchief after another back and forth across her thigh, placing the stretched fabric neatly in a pile to be ironed. In our home, the washerwoman, one of our three amahs, did this work. I went home that day, humbled and distraught. Cake and champagne suddenly seemed all wrong. I never visited her again.

A couple of years later, my father's financial situation spiralled out of control. When my mother came to my number two sister and I to say that she was emptying our passbook bank accounts, we simply nodded, stunned. We continued to live well enough, but the whispers in the night were loud in my head. I would remember my visit to my classmate upstairs, and how confused I felt that she seemed so happy, because I knew her family was, if not exactly poor, certainly not as well off as mine. The whispers told me that Mum was eating all the bitterness a Chinese wife could eat; not only did she have a philandering husband (the more bearable sorrow), now she also had to suffer a loss of face in her world while still propping up my father, who froze, unable to cope. Yet my mother continued to smile and act as if everything was fine. No one had to explain this very Chinese concept to me. My friend upstairs was evidence of that.

There's something fundamentally wrong with a culture where money is almighty, where face matters entirely too much, and where shame is inevitable if you cannot claim your standing in society. Which is why bidding HK goodbye is simply a necessary escape.

As a girl, a young teen, it was possible to live well without spending money we no longer had. In fact, it became a point of pride. After all, Mum made sure we had school fees, books, uniforms and food on the table. My second sister and I shared this forbidden knowledge of our penury that our two younger siblings could not yet understand; we stoically banished 'I want' from our vocabularies. What changed most for me was that I finally understood the true privilege of wealth, and bore a deep shame at my younger belief in Santa Claus, a belief that should have ended when I was eight, but which I stubbornly clung to despite the Incident of the Note in the Night.

When I was eight, my family flew first class on the British Overseas Airway Corporation to Singapore, where we spent Christmas. Both my number two sister and I were allowed to miss the last few days of school for this visit to our cousins, followed by a trip to Kuala Lumpur, Penang and Malacca. Number three sister was only four, but she came along as well, while our baby brother stayed home with our aunts. My sisters and I were excited, but our abiding concern was what would happen when Santa arrived with all our Christmas gifts.

Admittedly, I had begun to have my doubts about this reindeer-propelled fantasy, but did not want to confront the truth yet. Mum, bless her, sneaked our presents under our beds a few days before we left, along with a handwritten note, purportedly from Santa Claus, explaining that he knew we were going to Singapore and had decided to surprise us. Even though the handwriting suspiciously resembled Mum's, I brushed that aside. When your younger sisters can't care, you also won't. Among our gifts were Roman helmets, shields and swords; we couldn't wait to play with those when we came home from our trip.

But in school one day after this grand adventure, a

girlfriend called me a 'baby' for still believing in Santa Claus. Incensed, I offered this as proof to the contrary – Well we got helmets, shields and swords, and I saw those at Shui Hing department store and each set was over 200 dollars. Only Santa Claus could bring us something so expensive! Despite my protests, even then, I suspected she was right.

Now, older and less naive, as I watched my mother take and empty even our piggy banks, collecting small change to pay for our lives, I recalled my childish trucelence and understood how wealthy my father really must have been. How much he lavished on us. The crystal chandelier in our home; the stereo system imported from Germany; even our novelty telephone, a standing receiver with a dial on the base, a collectible today; the fancy dresses made from material from Whiteaways, an exclusive British department store; tickets for the best seats to see Dame Margot Fonteyn dance; the grand birthday parties and brunches or dinners at top restaurants – all these luxuries, unnecessary, frivolous, extravagant, afforded only by those who need never stop believing in Santa.

My more enlightened girlfriend came from a single-mother household and lived in a much smaller flat a few streets away with none of the trappings of my home. When we were in secondary school, she couldn't wait to leave school so she could get a job to earn a living.

She didn't go to university. That too was a luxury only for those with money, or blessed with superior intelligence.

Finally, I saw how far and hard had been Dad's fall from his perch.

Penury. I saw the beggars in the street with fresh eyes. There but for the grace . . . yet I was painfully aware how well off I still was, despite the dire pronouncements inside our home.

Besides, there were other distractions.

The greatest distraction of my teenage life was not the Legion of Mary (visiting ancient, impoverished women who spoke dialects I couldn't understand as a means of 'doing good works' eventually proved pointless), nor the drama club (theatre was not really my scene), nor piano lessons (these were expensive and, by the age of eleven, I knew I was not gifted enough to be a concert pianist), nor even the school newspaper. Instead, what kept my spirits occupied, for better or worse, was the Girl Guides.

Lord and Lady Baden Powell established what evolved into an international boys and girls movement that found its way to colonial Hong Kong. It is today a movement that invites mockery, given the homophobic attitudes and paedophilia scandals that colour its recent history. After all, there is evidence that Lord BP himself was a closeted gay man. Perhaps it is fortunate I never learned of this hypocrisy till much later, because my early teen years were riveted by this righteous movement – the marching, hoisting of colours, tying of knots, rope-throwing, stalking, campfire-making, pitching and striking of tents that we camped under till a typhoon washed us into surrender, hiking and map-reading. All these outdoor activities netted me badges of honour, and several indoor ones as well – reading, writing, playing hostess, cooking, embroidery. But acquiring Commonwealth Knowledge felt distressingly close to yet another history exam, so that badge I declined to attempt. It was the closest thing to a military conscription I would ever experience.

It was also wonderfully escapist. The camaraderie, the leadership roles (I was voted first as a Patrol Second, then a Patrol Leader and finally a Company Leader, which meant I could sew first one, then two and finally three white stripes on my breast pocket, a signal of honour to display), the rain-soaked nights under canvas tents at the top of Fei Ngo Shan, Flying Goose Hill. And, as puberty roiled, the possibility of dances with Boy Scouts. Be prepared was the motto we lived by. A good military is like that, full of mottos and credos and heroics to inspire, to distract you from the world as it is because the world as it should be is disciplined, controllable, with achievable goals for which you can be recognised. Obey and you, too, will belong in the club that counts.

But amid all that marching and singing and shining of brass trefoils, there was that other club.

My yee ma, or aunt, my mother's older sister, was an English teacher in the public schools. She drove a silver-blue Gordini, named after an Italian race car driver who also manufactured sports cars in France. I liked the shape of her car – less race car and more a sleekly practical form – and when memory speaks, it is this car that drives my childhood, even more than the succession of cars my parents owned, the black and white Dodge, Mum's white NSU, a deep red Valiant, that black Humber Hawk. The last was a replacement for the Valiant my father crashed one afternoon in the New Territories. For several years, whenever we drove out to Taipo or Fanling, we would look for the lamp post Dad destroyed in that accident, an icon of family lore.

But it is the Gordini with silver paint peeling off its inside door handles, a peeling I furthered, that drove me past that other club in the mornings.

During my early years, Auntie regularly drove my number two sister and me to school. She lived in our building on the twelfth floor and did not have a veranda. Her flat faced east and had a view of the Royal Observatory. A school teacher today would have a hard time affording an equivalent flat, never mind a car, but between herself and her lifelong companion, who worked as a secretary-translator at the Indonesian consulate, these two working girls could afford a reasonable life. At the time she taught at a girls' school in Kowloon City and could drop us off at Maryknoll's Boundary Street entrance. The drive took us along Nairn Road, renamed Princess Margaret Road after the 1966 royal visit. That road had one of HK's first flyovers, a raised roadway, a skyway that lifted us closer to the heavens. It excited me to ride up high because it gave me a view of the city I hadn't previously seen. In particular, we passed a school that was not like other schools. An image of Chairman Mao graced its exterior, and the Chinese Communist Party flag flew on its roof. From above, we could see the outdoor courtyard, surrounded on three sides by floors of classrooms. I gazed at this sight, so foreign in my city. China was this gigantic Big Six[16] 大陸 mainland next door, something I could only imagine from the hundreds of refugees landing on our shores each day, the freedom swimmers. Or the Yu Hwa department stores that sold goods from China, the stores we were warned not to enter. Or the communist movie theatres that showed propaganda films from the mainland. These all existed along the sightline of my childhood, but none as prominently as that school.

It was in the Gordini, early one morning as we drove past, that I briefly glimpsed that Red world in action. It

16 The second character, 陸, in the Chinese term for 'mainland' is a Cantonese homonym for 六, the number six, hence the pun.

was morning assembly, and all these Chinese students in their blue and white uniforms had lined up on the playground. At my Catholic school, morning assembly meant we – mostly Chinese – students were led in prayer, followed by the singing of hymns and the school song. Each student had a hymnal prayer book. Here, however, the students clutched a different book, one with a red cover that they raised in concert above their heads, chanting slogans of a different stripe. Up, down, up. And then we sped past. That sight, which I only glimpsed again a few times, nevertheless became an indelible memory. It also gave me my first inkling of the divided Chinese world I inhabited. These students were obviously not the children of those who favoured a British colonial education. Nor were they those who attended local Chinese-medium schools, which still counted as a colonial education, with children of all social classes, including the children of Nationalist Kuomintang sympathisers. Somewhere in British Hong Kong there had to be at least a few members of a Chinese Communist Party, or Chinese people whose politics leaned left. Their children had to go to school too.

Through my childhood and teenage years, years focused on self-centred concerns, years frittered away on fads, frivolities and the wastefulness of youth, this image stuck in my brain. A reminder, perhaps, that there always was that other club, the one to which I did not belong, the one my city did not embrace, understand or know, except in a superficial, meaningless fashion, dismissed in favour of our pragmatic, capitalist now, now, now, ignoring the inevitable tomorrow until the future becomes now.

Be prepared became my pessimistic anthem as the innocent years disappeared into oblivion, to be replaced by an inescapable future. A future for which HK is still, even now, unprepared.

III

Dear HK,
In this time before . . .

In 2015, an Indian summer lingers well into November. Every November since my second return to HK in 1992, my winter wardrobe remains unused. It is always an Indian summer now, predictable, no longer an aberration. In November 2015, I hosted the last speaker of the Pulitzer Writer Series, a program I've curated for the local university of my residence since my third return in 2010. This tenure has been an odd one, as writer-in-residence of their Department of English. No one seemed to notice that I moved in until 2015, when management opened an existential Pandora's Box, and, well, you can guess at what ensued.

As this particular year draws to a close, I am sanguine about the personal upheavals in my tiny corner of the Kowloon Peninsula. In 2010, I helped to establish Asia's first and, to date, only low-residency, international MFA in Creative Writing, at the university's request. It was a reason to return to HK a third time. On the one hand I was delighted because I believed in the value of such a program for Asia. Even so, I hesitated; the idea of a full-time faculty position at a university, especially if it meant having to live in Hong Kong, was not something I desired or sought. My teaching experience in one of the top low-residency MFAs in the US was a part-time situation, even when I was its faculty chair. But this was Hong Kong, the department head explained, and the only way to do this was to take the job. So I did, some-what reluctantly, propelled by the prospect of creating something innovative and new for the city of my birth.

Five years on, in March of this pivotal year, the university abruptly (and some say absurdly) closed the program, unleashing a protest by students, alumni, faculty and other international writers that was so globally loud that even the university's public relations department woke up and lumbered into damage control mode.

But I was telling you about a November Indian summer, and a Pulitzer finalist from Alaska who brought us her landscape of snow. The large lecture room at our Run Run Shaw Building[17] filled up. It was a surprising

---

17 Every university in this town has a building by Run Run, who is actually Sir Run Run Shaw, or 邵逸夫 (1907–2014). If you're truly a Hong Konger, you will bow to him as the ruler of the cultural heart of this city. Forget the Arts Development Council, or the ballet, symphony and foreign-influenced literary festivals. Forget the Trade Development Coun-cil's annual book fair, which is roughly 50 per cent text books, 45 per cent commercial

audience, not the usual suspects of glocalised readers, writers and lovers of literature, although those suspects occupied some of the seats. Instead, a number of younger Chinese students appeared in droves and listened, fascinated, to Eowyn Ivey's reading from her novel *The Snow Child*, this delightful retelling of a Russian fairy tale, this dark story of an old couple's desperate longings and desires, magically fulfilled for a brief time in 1920s Alaska. Literature is necessary to remind us we are human, to register our yearnings. There could not have been a better end to this era because a local university actually fulfilled its educational promise of innovative learning and a creative curriculum for a global world, even if, alas, only for a brief – too brief – while.

2015 has been a bad year for universities in HK. Many students protested at Occupy's Umbrella Revolution the year before, and the fallout lingers for them. At various institutions, protests and dramas were enacted around issues of corruption, decision-making procedures and transparency.[18] It appears that the youth of this city

---

literature and 5 per cent literature of cultural value. These attempts at glocalised local culture pale under the shadow of Sir Run Run Shaw. Founder of Shaw Brothers Studio, one of the largest film production companies in Asia, and TVB, Hong Kong's dominant television channel, this man from Ningbo began his career in Shanghai and Singapore before moving to our city in 1957. His philanthropy is legendary, and, notably, he funded education and the local creative arts initiatives, the latter focus being a rarity among those who make their money in Hong Kong.

18 At the University of Hong Kong, the school's council rejected the appointment of a pro-democracy law professor for a senior appointment, which stirred up huge controversy; at Baptist University, the university president refused to present degrees to any students who carried yellow umbrellas (the symbol of the Occupy movement) to the graduation ceremony; at City University of Hong Kong, a social science professor who was politically active and democratically inclined was demoted from chair professor to regular professor three months before his retirement (thus negatively affecting his retirement benefits)

believe in democracy, rule of law, freedom of information. How inconvenient, cringe the elder elite who run these institutions, those highly paid (some say overpaid) paper pushers and intellectuals. You can almost hear the senior stratum murmuring as they lounge on their various Mounts Olympi: Why can't students simply shut up, study and play like good little girls and boys?

As the year ends, I cannot dream of a white Christmas, as I must remain on these shores with my petulant lover. My dear John is angry with me, because I have chosen to depart on New Year's Day, turning my back on him in favour of Arizona's desert for the first several months of the new year. *Have you ever seen the desert in winter?* I say. *Flowers bloom, the sky is blue, days are warm and nights are comfortably chilly for excellent slumber.* But he will not listen to my 'pointless poetics', choosing instead to sulk, insisting that I cannot leave him again because who will help him, he grumbles, to locate his wallet, watch and keys, his passport or HKID, and all those other items and memories he regularly misplaces?

In 2015, the trouble with a lover like HK – this curmudgeonly younger man – is that he still shoulders

due to an 'investigation' about a supposedly plagiarised piece; at Lingnan University, one senior official resigned amidst allegations of plagiarism, and another, who applied for a leave, was accused of fast-tracking doctoral degrees at a private school in which he had a stake; at The Chinese University of Hong Kong, a council meeting was halted due to student protestors who demanded a voice in discussions on key appointments, since they presumably had doubts about how such appointments were being made. Yes, all of the above really did make local and even some international headlines in 2015 – you can't make this stuff up. The upshot of all this palaver is that the HK CE's official position as chancellor to all publicly funded universities is now an issue of ongoing concern.

the weight of patriarchal practices that really ought to be shucked. *Think oysters,* I say, but he lacks a sense of wordplay. *Hey, even Taiwan has a female president now,* I say, but that only irritates him more. You'd think he'd at least be happy for his Chinese cousin, that democratic Chinese nation-territory that is not yet a S.A.R., a Special Administrative Region, like us (assuming it will ever be 'granted' such status by its sovereign daddy, or is it mummy?). Assuming they would even want it.

Instead, his complexion glows greenish, envious of all Chinese and Asian territories more fortunate than he, more privileged than he, more courageous than he. *Happier than you,* I point out, because he is obsessed with reading surveys and statistics, because he simply doesn't read, not properly, certainly not literature, which might make him a little smarter and less self-obsessed. So I read to him from the latest survey, *47 per cent of women here are dissatisfied with their sex lives, behind Taiwan although we're at least ahead of Singapore,* thinking this perhaps will cheer him up. It doesn't, and I recall, too late, that his Singaporean lover dumped him for an Indian chap, which really incensed him. *Read this book,* I say, and hand him Dung Kai-cheung's brilliant novel *Atlas: The Archaeology of an Imagined City,* reminding him he can read it in his mother tongue, the *real* one, Cantonese, adding, *This Hong Kong fiction writer might teach you a thing or two about our city and history*. But he is peevish about language, never mind literature, since history barely registers in a city that forgets and expunges its inconvenient past. Inarticulate and inchoate, reassured only by business, science, technology, dining and shopping, he celebrates 'facts' that are more like fiction. HK thinks a tunnel-vision path is the only way to stay afloat and safe until 2047 and beyond. *Life isn't only about being safe,* I say, *you have to take risks.* But he's already rolled over and fallen asleep. His sleep is restless, nightmares outnumbering peaceful dreams. And he snores, his breathing laboured thanks to the polluted air.

In this supposedly post-feminist moment, it is exhausting to swaddle my tedious lover, one who cries and protests endlessly, believing himself entitled, as if all the world owes him the privilege of A Perfect Existence, entirely on his terms, forever unchanged.

More than a year after an Umbrella Revolution and the tented city life that occupied our streets, we still don't know who we are, what we are or how we want to be, arrested as we are in a state of permanent adolescence, waiting to be handed fare for the passage to adulthood.

(3)

Was it easier to be young in this city when I was young?

In 1970, the year I had to think about higher education, there were only two universities here, the University of Hong Kong and the Chinese University. It never occurred to me to apply to either, as my grades were far too poor. Besides, I did not want to attend Upper Six, the seventh year of secondary education required in our version of the British system, as that meant yet another public exam, the 'Matric', or A-levels, in order to compete for a local university place.

Since my father was virtually broke, and my academic performance middling to muddled, my choices were limited. I could forget the 'famous' universities, meaning expensive ones that everyone had heard of and would want to attend, such as Yale, Harvard, Stanford,

Princeton *et al.* In 1971, the year I was a freshman in college, those from Hong Kong who could attend such schools were either extremely wealthy, well connected or academically gifted; I was none of the above. A few years earlier, a distant cousin who was an academic whiz won a scholarship to Harvard without the aid of family money or connections. His achievement garnered several inches in the columns of local papers. Today, I'm not sure any media would care, given how many offspring of the local elite scamper down paved paths through expensive international schools towards such universities, regardless of academic aptitude. As delighted as our family was for my cousin, and despite my mother's fervent wish that one of us would perform likewise, it was clear that mine would be a very different path. You can buy tutors and fancy schools – even manipulate grades with generous donations. But if students do not really have the aptitude, and worse, lack the character to try, they won't amount to a hill of beans (perhaps a knoll of tofu, at most), regardless of parental wealth, connections or constant cajoling.

If memory speaks honestly, as it does if you pay attention, I basically left my higher educational fate to desire and chance.

Desire is a powerful force, especially when you're sixteen, certain that escape from the city of your birth is your one hope for salvation. Desire is also melodramatic, a trait I shared at the age of sixteen, but I was aware of how highly privileged that desire was because my parents were able to imagine a foreign university life for me. She never had to say so, but it was clear that Mum expected me to do whatever was necessary to go. She just couldn't quite tell me where to go or how to do it, except by instilling in me just enough discipline, fear of failure, independence and ambition to make something of my life. Besides, she had other concerns, like looking after my younger siblings, juggling family finances and keeping up appearances for a husband who had sunk into a prolonged depression. Dad said a lot less about all this. His humiliation at having to borrow money from my aunts, which my mother did so that the family could eat, silenced him for a very long time.

But Dad could still write a letter to America, which he did.

To complicate Tolstoy with Chinese characteristics: *Every diaspora Chinese family is unhappy in its own particular way, but will have a relative in some promised land to offer useful advice.*[19] Mine appeared in the form of my father's older first cousin, whom Dad had not seen since they were boys in Tegal. This was his super smart cousin with the photographic memory and amazing

---

19 By definition, members of a diaspora Chinese family are guaranteed to be unhappy at least some, if not all, of the time, as they regularly ingest vast amounts of bitterness. This allows them to live up to the stereotype that to be a global Chinese is to swallow and choke on bitterness, as we're tediously reminded to 吃苦, or to endure as much hardship as is humanly possible.

IQ (since every extended Chinese family simply has to have at least one intellectual genius per generation), the first to land permanently in the US. He had earned a PhD, established a professional career and married an American with whom he was raising four children, all of which were great credentials. But he was, essentially, a stranger. By contrast, my father's two brothers who were not strangers also held PhDs and were professors in Canada. Which meant I was duty bound to consider Canada, and did so by submitting an application to McGill upon entering Lower 6, only to be rejected because Canada required Upper Six, which I knew full well. It was half-hearted, that application, because I didn't want to go to Canada. Or England. Or even the West Coast of the US, and especially not California, because every HK student went there. My ambition was to escape Hong Kong, British rule and local Canto culture in that order. Other than that, it was not at all clear to me why I was going to university, as the theoretical degree, job and career that would result were vague, unspecific goals. All I knew was that I very much wanted to do this, and also that wherever I ended up, I wished for it to be to somewhere with the fewest reminders as possible of my birth city.

In the wistfully sentimental song 'When You Wish Upon A Star', the lyrics at the bridge begin, 'Fate is kind.' *Be careful of what you wish for* has become a truism for my life's unpredictable path. I submitted only a handful of applications, selecting (out of a huge number, naturally) universities that offered a BA in English in cities that sounded exotic but would not be as crime-ridden as New York or Chicago – Minneapolis, for instance, where Mary Tyler Moore was a writer on her eponymous TV show; and Xavier University in Cincinnati, because it was run by Jesuits who, like the Maryknoll sisters at my school, were known to be liberal educators. I never properly consulted a map of the United States when making these choices. Instead I spent hours at the Institute of International Education, poring over giant directories of colleges and universities, trying to imagine – by reading between the lines – what a university education should encompass, making my decisions based on cost of tuition and the scope of courses offered. I badly wanted to study all that sounded glamorous and grand – Literature, Drama, Philosophy, Political Science, Psychology – subjects that had minimal space in my secondary curriculum. Meanwhile, my parents argued over money as I sat for the SAT and TOEFL.[20] Afterwards, I studied the fine print on the I-20 forms received from these institutions when they accepted me for study.

20 The acronyms stand for the Scholastic Aptitude Test and Test of English as a Foreign Language respectively. The first required practice tests because the logic of the English was American and peculiar, although the math was easy, making me feel, for the first time in my life, competent in math. The latter felt like an insult, since English was not a foreign language for me, although once I landed on American shores I was to be disabused of that notion, as post-sixties American English – with its multitude of slang words and linguistic evolution of the twentieth century – proved to harbour a diction and articulation that was far, far more foreign than any English I ever knew.

The problem was money.

Fate is, at best, only conditionally kind. Dad wrote that letter to his cousin, my American uncle as I would eventually come to think of him, to ask for advice. My uncle lived near a small state college where, he said, scholarships were being offered to attract foreign students. I applied because a financial reality loomed, but did so reluctantly because the college sounded too small to be interesting and had neither Mary Tyler Moore nor Jesuits to recommend it. The scholarship offer arrived – this was no great achievement as the numbers of foreign students who applied were few and my SATs and TOEFL scores were good – and sealed my fate.

So I got my wish: Plattsburgh, New York was as different and distant from Hong Kong as possible. There were only five other female Chinese students out of around 120 foreign students in the student body of approximately 3000. Even though the courses offered were not as varied or glamorous as those at the University of Minnesota, and even though the college was less exclusive than Xavier University appeared to be, I did get to study enough that was new, including World Politics and Reader's Theatre. I also read Emily Dickinson, e. e. cummings, Dorothy Parker, Marguerite Duras *et al,* just a few of the authors who would prove influential to my own development as a writer. My English and French were good enough to test me out of a semester's worth of freshman year credits, thus saving money by shortening my time as a student. In summers I slung pizza or balanced cocktails at restaurants, dusted souvenirs and rang up purchases in tourist shops. During the school year I worked on campus as a resident counsellor in exchange for a free dorm room plus part of my board. Within three years, I had completed a BA, returned to Hong Kong and immediately received offers for several good jobs, despite my 'useless' degree in English from some unknown college (*Where did you say you went again?*) in America.

So I suppose it was easier to be young when I was young because there were fewer expectations. A higher degree, even if not from an ivy league or top university, still assured you a job and a reasonable career. It was not necessary to pre-determine your future and force yourself into law, medicine, business, engineering or technology if your talents, desires and inclinations were not served by such ambitions or careers. Even my limited language skills – fluent only in English – were not a hindrance. It was still possible to succeed to your family's satisfaction and contribute to society. I could even lessen the financial burden on my parents so that my younger siblings could also afford university.

What I envy of young people today is the ease with which they own the world. Those young people who could be me forty years ago – meaning those who are either somewhat 'foreign' or who go abroad to study – fly home every holiday, which was unaffordable when I was a student. They talk to the world on their cellphones; I spoke to my parents only twice by international long distance during all my undergraduate years. Most enviable, however, is their access to what's happening around the world. It is not about money but technology. The young are more privileged than I was because they can be, if they choose, far more knowledgeable than I could be. But if the seeds of my discontent were sown by what little I did know of the world, is it any surprise that young Hong Kongers today, given their greater knowledge, would explode in protest the way I did not have to in my day?

So yes, it was easier to be young when I was young because even though my city was less wealthy, less cosmopolitan, less first world than it is now, I knew it had a future. If this is an elegy, it is for the loss of the future of my city.

My life exploded whenever I left HK, scattering pieces of me around the world. At seventeen, my tears over leaving home were quickly replaced by the wonder of the new, of all that Hong Kong did not offer.

Most of all, I discovered how little I knew, how constrained an outlook my birth city had given me. Had I been more Chinese, I probably would have been better educated, because I would at least have had a network of teachers and classmates who could have shared books and ideas with me. If nothing else, I would have been properly schooled in Chinese culture, history and literature. Instead, I was stuck in that no-person's land, betwixt the local and the expatriate, neither fish nor fowl. My parents had hardly any local friends. Nor did they have many British and certainly no American friends. All I knew of the country I wanted to go to was the language and a mixed bag of pop and real culture. And once I arrived, I realised how little I actually understood about the culture and even the language. The colonial education Hong Kong offered me was dauntingly limited because there was a lack of context for all the foreign concepts it contained. Which is why, I believe, the sciences and mathematics hold such sway over my city, because these subjects contain objective knowledge that does not typically require cultural reference.

It is only now, when we are postcolonial and hybrid, and have adopted an origin-less flower, the bauhinia, as the city's symbol, that all this explosive unknowing has started to become knowable.

But in 1974, when I returned home unhappily, left with no other choice unless I chose to attend graduate school, HK was still a mystery to me.

Another truth, universally acknowledged, is that a young woman in possession of a degree will look for and expect to get a job. It did not occur to me at the time, no doubt due to my lopsided education, that a young woman might also seek the right husband with a requisite fortune to provide for her. For one thing, in 1974 when I was twenty, I had become accustomed to making my own living.

Among my former school friends, including those who also went abroad for university, I was odd. For one thing, I returned a year too soon, because I had completed my BA in just three years. And for another, I was not interested in the 'right' jobs. The position as a lecturer in English, for example, at an institution of higher education. What I had discovered in studying for my BA was that universities offered limited life experience. And the idea of a PhD felt like far too much school, which was why I declined to enter the University of Utah, though I had applied to and been accepted into a doctoral studies program in Milton. There are many things I've regretted about my youth, but skipping out on the PhD is not one. I would likely not be a writer today if I had gone down that path. Likewise, even though my mother very much wanted me to either go on for my PhD or accept the local lecturer position, I declined, because it felt like time for me to leave the cosseted environment of school and figure out the real world.

My first return to HK was lonely. School friends who went abroad had not yet returned. A few friends who hadn't gone to university were around, but many got married within a few years, usually to foreigners, and migrated abroad. My friends were mostly the foreign girls of my secondary school life – Portuguese, primarily – who gravitated towards Western men as mates.

Meanwhile, after three years abroad on my own, I was living at home and hating it. During those years away, I had lost my virginity, gotten violently drunk, smoked pot, hash and too many cigarettes, and studied creative writing. All these acts sealed my status as a misfit in HK. My head was filled with Marguerite Duras, Emily Dickinson, Dorothy Parker and Milton. To make matters worse, I actually liked sex (it would later astonish me how many women did not) and had had a couple of grand romances. The boys I loved were bartenders or wanderers – one Romeo hitchhiked across the country – and were Puerto Rican, Brazilian, Czech, Indian, black American and the odd white American. This was not a great dating history in a city where girls lived pretend-virginally at home, got respectable jobs as teachers or pink-collar professionals, and dated nice Chinese boys on a parallel masculine track, from among whom they eventually chose one to marry.

There were not many other women like me in HK.

HK was conservative, rigid, and without a space for creative writers. The HK Cantonese poet Leung Ping-kwan once said of being a writer in this city that 'one better does it with the understanding that this place does not believe in "architects of the souls", as the old socialist phrase goes, that it doesn't provide much space for artistic development'. Unfortunately, I was not to meet PK till years later, in 1996 in Berlin, just as I did not meet any other HK writers till much later. There just was no real literary culture, and I did not have access to the local universities where a microscopic amount of artistic endeavours occasionally occurred. And of course, I was not Chinese enough, otherwise I probably would have found other writers like PK who were around back then, just as I would have known about and read the writing from China, Taiwan and Hong Kong, all the work that was not yet translated but available in Chinese.

But meanwhile, I needed to get a job.

When memory speaks of my life as a fresh graduate, the loudest whisperers surround my family's insular foreignness. I bumbled into jobs in much the way I bumbled into university: a convergence of chance and desire. It was years before I realised that others sought and found assistance from their local connections, waiting for the 'right' position while living for awhile at home without employment. This was not an option for me. My world comprised three things: the urgent need to earn a living, since my parents were still somewhat broke; an eagerness to work; and a burning desire for independence.

From where did I get such a need for independence? This startles me now when I consider how dependent a territory HK is. We grow and harvest nothing; we do not raise animals for food; these days we no longer even make much of anything, and what we did make contributed only to frivolity and waste – plastic flowers, disposable toys, cheap clothing and shoes to be worn and discarded. We have become a knowledge economy, I hear, but does the knowledge to incessantly buy and sell – property, shares, gambling bets – really amount to much more than a knoll of tofu? We fool ourselves, frantically scrambling through life in our city, trading jobs for the highest position, yet we are entirely dependent on a place and economy that is more air than substance. A 'career' never struck me as a serious consideration during this first return to HK. Instead, I opened the want ads in the *South China Morning Post* and looked for a job that paid.

My first salaried job (I worked briefly in sales for commission only) was at a small printing company. Their clientele was largely law and accounting firms, and the primary product was inexpensive and quick printing of shelf company memoranda and articles of association. The account servicing office was in Central's Gloucester Building, a colonial relic long since demolished. Each weekday morning, a man in a uniform and white gloves would pull open the gate of the ancient lift to ferry me to my floor, where I, the first one in, would unlock the door and open our two-room office for business. On the days I was late, I would have to shamefacedly acknowledge the staff, patiently waiting outside for their irresponsible 'boss' to show up. I was rarely late after the first time.

The problem, of course, was that I had no business being any kind of boss. At twenty, with only a BA to my name, my work experience as a dorm counsellor, waitress and summer resort junk store sales clerk should not have qualified me for anything. The full staff consisted of one layout artist, one final art production artist, a typist-cum-typesetter who worked on an IBM Selectric with two font choices, and a print operator who ran the AB Dick offset machine. Everyone else was older than I was and had real experience at their respective trades; the final art production artist was a man old enough to be my father. The staff rarely called in sick, showed up on time and worked. My job was to be traffic cop – jobs came in, I organised and logged them into the register, and then I farmed them through the system. At the end of each day, I had to complete the bookkeeping records in the Kalamazoo accounting system the company used, a large, blue hardcover ledger book that mimicked computerised accounting because a single entry would copy its way through to the other pages of records. It was my introduction to balancing books. Office hours were 9:30 a.m. to 6:30 p.m. Monday to Friday, with a half-day on Saturday mornings. Occasionally, because I spoke good English, I would accompany the English owner of the company and his office manager, a smart Chinese woman who had been his secretary and was now his business partner, to visit clients for whom the language of commerce was English. My business card read 'Account Executive'.

But the job was salaried, beginning around HK$750 a month plus a bonus as a percentage of the business our office handled; I usually managed to make around $850 to $900 a month. In today's dollars, this would be the equivalent of around $9000 or $10 000, a salary many fresh graduates considered beneath them until the economy tanked and their choices shrank. Also, while the company was neither large nor prestigious, it was on the cutting edge of a revolution in printing, as this was long before ubiquitous photocopying, desktop computers and instant printing. When memory speaks, I realise that it was a privilege for me to do this job, in which I learned administrative skills, client servicing and the management of deadlines for projects. It was a privilege to have been given such trust, offered work experience and paid.

My rent (because by then I had moved to a small house in Sha Tin) was $500 a month, which I shared with my boyfriend. We only had cold running water, a squat toilet, a makeshift shower and one large-ish room.

No telephone because the phone company did not have lines out that far. My commute, by bus and the Star Ferry, took me around an hour one way, longer if I had to stop at the market on the way home. We certainly never had a domestic helper. For me it was as good a start to an independent life as was possible.

Perhaps one reason it is easy to bid farewell to HK is that my attitude towards work and life seems seriously outdated in my city. A job is a privilege. Why anyone should hire a know-nothing twenty-year-old to do anything still astounds me. In the US, I considered my first waitressing job a privilege because I had never picked up a serving tray in my life. During my three summers working at restaurants and souvenir stores, I had to earn my bosses' trust if I wanted to return to work the next summer. The same was true for my first HK job. While all workers should and do have rights, I still believe that you do not bite the hand that feeds you until the hand proves itself unworthy of wielding that power. My earliest HK employer was not perfect, but the company was responsibly managed, job expectations were clear and we were paid regularly. For what more should a young person ask?

Or is it that employers, and employees as well, are not as worthy as they once were? My last 'prestigious' employer in HK, a large public university, proved to be by far the least ethical and most irresponsible employer of my entire professional career. Likewise, a number of employees at all levels I encountered there displayed a shocking disregard for job responsibilities, despite their excellent pay. Absenteeism was high. Even in the actual English department, the standard of English among university graduates and post-graduate students was shockingly low. The secretary-office manager at the printing company did not have a university degree, but wrote and spoke English at a significantly higher standard than many local colleagues at the university. These complaints are not a memory of the city but a portrait of it today.

IV

Dear HK,
Why fight?

Chinese New Year 2016 has gotten off to a rough start. From my cottage in the Arizona desert, I follow news of the latest riot in Mongkok, as well as the ensuing argument in HK media about whether or not this really is a riot. Comparisons are drawn to the 1966 riots and the echoes of social unrest then, when the British were the bad guys. There's always a bad guy for HK to fight, and the problem, always, is about the desire for political self-determination that simply is not in the make-up of the city's character.[21] Oh it's there in fits and starts, but HK is such a petulant young thing, lacking a central focus for his life. Expediency has trumped all for so long that it's now second nature.

21 My short story 'Democracy' (*History's Fiction*, Chameleon Press, 1st ed. 2001; 2nd ed. 2005) is set against the sixties unrest and details the ill-fated course of democratic elections for a group of teenage girls in their Girl Guide company. It is loosely based on my own experience, and was the closest thing to true democracy I ever witnessed (or am, sadly, likely to witness) in my birth city.

Am I too harsh, am I unkind? It's difficult to be fair to a lover who has lost his lustre. Perhaps it is because this lover too closely resembled an arranged marriage by Daddy Britain and Mummy China. Or is that parental gender pairing the other way around? Maybe it is a same sex couple after all, now that we've entered the enlightened twenty-first century. In any event, my entanglement with HK has long been contested, an uneasy truce one day, a passionate embrace the next. Passion flares and dies quickly – an uneasy truce has greater longevity.

Be quiet, I want to tell the city, *and content yourself with the expedient decisions you've chosen for your existence.* The problem is, the natives are restless, and HK has reason to worry, even while pretending that the cake will rise and expand enough to feed everyone for a long, long time.

Hush, I say, *HK you simply were never the place to nurture and grow a writer.*

In the end, that is the reason to leave, because this writer cannot fit inside her skin in the HK of pragmatism and profit, the two Ps that trumps all else, including common sense, until the restless and beleaguered hearts shout, *Enough!*

(4)

My first return to HK lasted almost seven years, from the summer of 1974 to the autumn of 1981, before the itch to leave again set in. Technically, I was gone for almost a year from mid-1980, roaming around Central Greece and the islands when the drachma was considerably cheaper than the Euro, and rooms of my own housed me near London and also in Paris, where being down and out was both *de rigueur* and Orwellian. When memory speaks of those early adult years, it is travel away from HK that is recalled with the greatest pleasure. Which makes me wonder if home is really where the heart is, or where you simply park your stuff during specific time periods.

George Carlin, who died in 2008, gave us the greatest discourse on stuff. Many of my early years involved the acquisition and disposal of stuff, which was and still is relatively easy in HK. The problem is, of course, housing, which has always been scarce, unless you're willing to take the road much less travelled out to the wilds of the New Territories. By standards, I have lived in vast HK spaces. In my family's home, which relocated to a flat in Kowloon Tong on what was then an inhospitable hilltop, my private space was the upper bunk bed in a tiny room shared with my brother. The flat was, however, modern and comfortably large – a little under 112 square meters for a family of six. My father's financial collapse necessitated the move out of our penthouse flat by the harbour, or so Mum insisted, because it could command a high rent. In 1970, my parents purchased the new suburban flat on a hilltop with no public transport. It cost HK$100 000, which today would barely get you a parking space. The developer palmed off these newly constructed spaces, and in time, this home has evolved into an overpriced 'luxury flat' because of its location. Which is laughable. The construction quality is shoddy – peeling paint, leaking roofs, carrying sounds; the plumbing atrocious – narrow pipes backing up sinks and toilets; noise from the highway behind us incessant; the car park design an Escher-esque nightmare. Only the constant shoring up and renovation over the years by the owners' association has made the building habitable. Bruce Lee died in our building, its one notable historic moment. Compared to our solid concrete block by the harbour, this was like moving into a shanty with sheen.

Which was partly why, after my first return to Hong Kong, I shacked up with the first foreign boyfriend I could stand to live with out in the wilds of Sha Tin. Later, we moved even further out beyond Sai Kung, where HK$1000 a month got us an entire two-storey house and outdoor space.

*

Jobs were plentiful, unlike in the US where a recession was in play. Lady Luck shone on my HK life, and lucre arrived with each roll of the dice. Following the printing company I landed a job as an English copywriter at a small ad agency, a branch of one of the larger 4A's, and a member of the American Association of Advertising Agencies. The company was in Causeway Bay, where their offices were situated in two converted residential flats. In 1976, Causeway Bay was still very residential, much less the congested commercial hub it is now. Daimaru was its centre, the first Japanese department store in HK, and later McDonald's opened its first location there. The larger ad agencies, however, were still in Central, as was most of the business and commercial life.

I loved the creative environment. We worked long hours to meet deadlines, but otherwise work was flexible.

I could wear jeans instead of a skirt and pantyhose, which was a throwback to my US college life. The boss was an enlightened HK Chinese man, one of the best bosses I ever worked for. Once, the entire office came to my Sha Tin home, the art director bearing a live chicken that he later slaughtered, plucked and cooked. The company threw us dinners for all the Chinese festivals, where we played mah-jong or poker and ate well. We parodied and joked about ridiculous clients; during downtime in the office, we talked about art, poetry and literature, in between writing commercials and ads. The work was stimulating and the vibe suited me.

Except that it wasn't literature or art.

I quickly discovered that the problem with wanting to be a real writer was that I couldn't write commercial creative work. Journalism I had already dismissed, as news reporting, with its manic *now now now* deadlines struck me as spectacularly deadening, and as attractive as feature writing seemed, it simply wasn't fiction. I had at first thought writing ad copy would be fine. After all, John Cheever, John Updike and Evan S. Connell among many other fiction writers had been the 'mad men' who wrote ad copy. But Hong Kong wasn't New York, where literary endeavours could co-exist with a day job, and where a literary life and publishers abounded. The *most* creative life I could hope to have in Hong Kong was in advertising.

This was the only time in my life when I actually stopped writing fiction. I do not experience writer's block as a rule, but turning out ad copy daily stymied my literary work. It is hard to be a good copywriter, just as it is to be a fiction writer, and I could not do both well. Literary fiction exercised the stronger pull, and eventually I had to acknowledge this truth.

And so, eighteen months later, I left and went to the client side in the form of a marketing position at a local airline.

In 1977, the airline was a large one in the region, but puny by international standards. They did not even have a 747 in the fleet when I entered the company, and I easily memorised the route map and its regional destinations. The long hauls – to Australia, and later to the Middle East – were serviced by 707s. The entire marketing division filled one small section of the fifth floor of the since-demolished-and-rebuilt office building, and comprised just ten people. We reported through department managers to an Australian general marketing manager. Our annual advertising budget was considerable in 1978, the year I was promoted to advertising superintendent, at a time when there wasn't even an advertising department.

Did I say the luck of my HK life depended on serendipity? My entry into the airline industry was due to a chance encounter with a human resources manager, a fortuitous back-door opening in marketing administration that was not advertised, and the maverick personality of the Australian in charge. He had fathered four girls and believed in hiring unconventional women (and men) to work under the British managers foisted upon him. During my tenure I worked for a wide variety of bosses, including two close-to-retirement managers who favored long lunches; one extremely bright and capable man whose rise was limited because he had married a Filipino (racism was overt); one extremely intelligent and likable man whose career was truncated by addiction; and one rising star whose tenure in marketing was brief because he was promoted to company secretary after only three months.

The marketing division I first stepped into was vibrant, fun and completely unconventional, and it was under this manager that the global advertising campaign featuring multinational flight attendants was first launched, a campaign that today might be considered sexist, and hence commercial suicide. Along with that were all the promotional tie-ups – Rugby Seven-a-Side, golfing, hot air balloons, dragon boat races, promotional giveaways and the like – as well as connections with tourism boards and top hotels in the region. Also, the airline was growing; new routes and services were being added. It was a job with a future, and my parents were delighted that I was finally employed at a prestigious company with good pay and benefits, travelling around the region on business (even occasionally further afield to London and San Francisco), and scoring free and discounted air tickets for my vacations to the US, Europe, Australia and Asia. Plus, my parents benefited from discounted tickets as well. More significantly, my position finally gave them bragging rights within their overseas Chinese diaspora.

Most important of all, I could write fiction again.

The travel was stimulating, and regular office hours allowed for an early morning and weekend writing routine. Three weeks of paid vacation, plus HK's famously numerous public holidays, meant that real work only happened around ten months out of the year. You could also count on typhoons regularly shutting down the office. Besides, this was advertising as a client, without the agency world that sapped my creative juices; all I really had to do was administer, check invoices, write a few memos and show up to work. As one senior local who had joined the company as a clerical staff years earlier told me, *My job is to move the pile of paper from my in tray to the out tray. In, out, in, out, it's all about moving the paper.*

By all measures, it should have been an ideal life for a writer.

The problem – isn't there always a problem? – was

that I was young, idealistic, and now even ambitious for some kind of professional career in addition to being a writer. Working at this large, prestigious company was a lesson in business reality, because when the universe is corporatised, profit trumps all. Even that was less daunting, however, than the machinations of the Hierarchy of Power.

In short, the problem was my not being a princess.

The fairy tale of the princess and the pea is instructive. A real princess, we are told, will feel even a single pea through a pile of mattresses because she is so sensitised by luxury that she can't possibly sleep the sleep of the proletariat. That is essentially the non-moral of the Hans Christian Anderson tale about a prince who can't find a *real* princess because his options are either too ugly, too fat, too rude or too uncultivated. The winning candidate, like Cinderella, must simply display the right shoe size or correct breeding. Obviously, she must also be classically beautiful, which the bruised pea princess is.

In fact, when I ponder the problems confronting HK's government at the moment, it strikes me that a form of royalty prevails among the governing class, one that is too far removed from the ordinary citizenry.

To digress into the present for a moment, a recent tirade by an ordinary woman at a LegCo meeting in February 2016 was recorded and uploaded on

YouTube. It immediately went viral. Beginning with a plea for a retirement scheme, she pointed out that even contaminated vegetables were now unaffordable. Her accusations rained down upon a government official who earned over HK$300 000 a month, yet said that a monthly salary of a mere $16 000 was very good. In particular, the woman listed the questionable incomes earned or extravagant expenditures by key top officials, ending each anecdote with the refrain, *No investigation*. Her central complaint was, *Are you kidding, is this the best you can do?* Her excoriation of the current government is an indictment of the social hierarchy that is rooted in HK's nature, even when memory speaks from almost forty years earlier.

How does HK shut you out? Let me count the ways.

The airline I worked for was formerly a cargo airline that had eventually been merged into a division of a large conglomerate. The way I saw it, there were then basically three paths to power. The English could enter the ranks of princelings who were primarily Oxbridge graduates from the right backgrounds (there was one Durham guy but he was the exception, as was the sole woman). Hong Kong Chinese entered as management trainee princelings, graduates of either Hong Kong or Chinese University, although a few graduates from acceptable (meaning, prestigious) American universities had begun to trickle in by then, as did one woman. Outside of these paths, it often felt as if the only way to power was through patience, long service and the eventual rise to management in the services or sales areas – flight attendants, airport ground staff, customer service, engineering, human resources, marketing and tour sales. Pilots were the exception: they ruled their own caste.

I was definitely not a princess, and patience was the least of my virtues.

One local Chinese colleague, I discovered, would raid his wealthy father's liquor cabinet and produce expensive bottles of champagne for our consumption. One Cambridge princeling scored tickets to dinner theatre, which he shared with me because I adored Noel Coward and knew his plays. The only two women filled me in on the sexual inequities of our benefits. British princesses did not get housing once they married because it was assumed their husbands would provide; unlike the men, HK Chinese princesses were simply never entitled to housing benefits in the first place.

What determined my future path in the end came from two sources: the *Harvard Business Review* and a conversation I had with a stranger in Greece.

This was the era of the MBA. A colleague told me I should get one. My father did not believe in the study of business, but his track record did not make him an authority. One day, a *Harvard Business Review* landed on my desk, the way magazines of all kinds appeared in my in tray thanks to my responsibility for advertising. While this was not exactly a journal in which the airline would choose to advertise, the case studies and articles did give me a sense of what the MBA might entail. It was an education for me, to discover what other paths my life could take, even if it felt jarring for a literary life. But I'm a writer, so I read anything and everything until I figure out what I don't need or want to read.

This was also the era before many HK folks travelled as easily as I could. Which was how I ended up in Greece. No one from Hong Kong went there, not even our airline employees. The Greek airlines were only too glad to give me free tickets – a perk of my job in marketing – because flights from Hong Kong were never full. Greece was popular with Europeans and some North Americans, but in Asia it was too foreign and faraway unless you were Japanese. I was that odd beast, a writer and reader of literature. Homer and *The Odyssey* swirled in my consciousness, alongside the mythology peppered through the traditions of English literature. Byron died there. Slouching towards Athens and Crete on holiday was almost inevitable.

In Syntagma Square one afternoon, I was sipping

coffee in the autumn sunshine when I struck up a conversation with an American fiction writer.

The year was 1979. Hong Kong was rapidly changing. We had an ICAC and a subway, the Mass Transit Railway or MTR. Seven years earlier, Nixon had gone to China, the first US president to set foot in the country under Communism. A year prior, Carter formally recognised China, and suddenly my city was invaded by American journalists, academics, business and leisure travellers en route to the mainland. I had married and divorced. I was also writing my first attempt at a novel set in Hong Kong, *Proximity*, about 1997 and what might transpire when a handover came to pass.[22] Although this was sometime before the Joint Declaration or any political clarity for our future, the writer in me considered the proximity of that deadline the most urgent question for a novelist. But there was hardly anyone I could talk to

22 Two versions of the novel manuscript exist, radically different, both stored in the library of City University of Hong Kong. The library asked for my papers just when I was about to burn all my old unpublished and published manuscripts, but their horrified response changed my mind. Both versions of the novel were read at various publishers in London and New York, all of who expressed interest, but in the end contemporary HK as a literary artifact was just not a thing that seemed to need to exist, which is why most of the novels set in Hong Kong tend to be genre rather than literary, penned by outsiders who gaze longingly and lovingly at history, criminal activity, prostitution and other exotica that stir the expatriate's imagination. Today, young writers emerging from Hong Kong write about, from or within it with far greater clarity. Two younger English-language poets from these shores recently won major international prizes for their work – Nicholas Wong was awarded the 2016 Lambda Literary Prize for poetry for his second book, *Crevasse*, and Sarah Howe won the 2015 T.S. Eliot prize in poetry for her debut collection, *Loops of Jade*. It delights me to see such achievements, because both these poets and other young writers I've read bring contemporary Hong Kong into sharp relief through literary excellence, as opposed to pandering only to commercial demands. If I and other writers who came before had to tread a longer and lonelier road, at least I have lived to witness the truth I knew as a young writer, that Hong Kong ought not be merely fetishised, orientalised, exoticised or otherwise resized to suit the bias of the Anglo publishing world. So it's okay if my first attempts at writing about my city remain forever unpublished. The fact that some library here cares enough to archive my papers is more than sufficient reward, way more than I ever dreamed possible.

about this. The writers I knew were mostly journalists whose attention was on the now. A novel was fanciful, not the stuff of their work. The only novelist I met was Derek Maitland, who had authored *The Only War We've Got,* and he generously gave me a helpful critique of my manuscript. But he also made a living as a journalist, which wasn't my path. There was no one to show me how to live a writer's life.

So that afternoon in Athens, as the sun crossed the sky into evening, this American writer who looked a little like Hemingway conversed with me for hours about writing and the writing life. And then he told me about the MFA.

The Masters of Fine Arts or MFA in creative writing had by then been established in the US a little over forty years earlier at the University of Iowa. In academic terms, it was still a relatively new degree. In England, the first MA in creative writing at the University of East Anglia was only nine years old. Despite the one creative writing course I had completed during my BA, no one at my university ever mentioned the possibility of such a graduate degree. Neither of the universities in Hong Kong had anything similar to offer.

When I returned from vacation, I considered the MFA versus the MBA, because by then I had been exploring the possibility of an executive MBA at Harvard, for which I could possibly get tuition reimbursed by my employer.

When memory speaks, the romance of the Hemingway lookalike from Arizona is unforgettable. In later years, I tried to track him down but never succeeded. The fleeting encounters of youth are careless, and serendipity is just that. You meet, you part, and your life changes forever. Names are uttered and forgotten, just as lovers you pick up and discard over the years no longer leave an imprint on your skin. The colleague who suggested the MBA was possibly a rich princeling – memory is also fickle and unreliable – a dual national British-American of mixed race who was himself headed towards the MBA. At least I think he was. He was pragmatic and helpful, but Arizona Hemingway flicked on a switch in my imagination that would not be extinguished.

Besides, profit is boring.

Each day at the main headquarters of the airline, the system-wide load factor of the previous day would click into a rotator display placed high up for all to see: 67 per cent, 72 per cent, 71 per cent. These numbers led to all kinds of analysis and programs for profit. My favourite was the YIP, the Yield Improvement Program, which triggered outbursts of hilarity among the princelings. Thus, the Marco Polo program was born, which landed in my inbox as instructions to get data crunched and mileage rules defined. But my mind could not entirely wrap itself around such logic. Balancing the passenger mix between high- and lower-yield travellers obsessed management.

That, and the frighteningly unpredictable price of oil, since the 1973 oil crisis was still a recent horror.

Yet what increasingly obsessed me was the shifting balance of power in the world as China peeked out from behind its bamboo curtain. That, and the proximity of the year 1997. The novel I had begun and was trying to write compelled me far more than the profitability of the airline. Also, a new advertising manager had been named, and my new boss looked askance at my bare legs (pantyhose were seriously demented in my view if you lived in a subtropical climate), the ambitions I expressed for promotion to assistant manager (good girls don't make demands), as well as my lack of princess heritage (pea, what pea?). My insistence on using Ms as opposed to Miss also did not go over well. When I questioned the unequal terms of employment for men and women, he dismissed such concerns as irrelevant. After all, he argued, *Your husband will look after you.* I begged to differ and pointed out my divorced state, which further rendered me socially defective.

The day I handed in my resignation, my HK boss was shocked. His expression said it all: *Why would anyone throw away such a good job?* What will you do, he asked. I did not have another job, so I told the truth: I planned to return to Greece to travel and write while applying for the MFA. His complete lack of comprehension told me I had made the right decision.

So there it was. I left HK the second time because there was no room to live a writer's life. My future was not only about money or a respectable career or conforming to the Hierarchy of Power. Profit is not a sufficient motivation for the human condition, even though it does provide impetus for many, especially in HK. Had I stayed at the airline, I might have eventually risen through the ranks. I might even eventually have self-published a vanity book – perhaps as my graceful retirement project – and all the princes and princesses would show up, congratulate me and purchase a copy for me to sign, although most probably wouldn't read it. The whole affair would be merely about social standing and profit, neither of which are reason enough to write.

It would be eleven years before I returned to HK to stay a second time. Those eleven years were how I finally became a writer, for real.

V

Dear HK,
Enough!

Sometimes, as the cruellest month nears, in the silence of the desert at night when it's daylight back in HK, I try to hear the voices of my city's youth amid all the tumult. The young are an alien race, their song from some distant galaxy, but in between the shockwaves of protests and shouts, a single note resounds: *Enough, enough, enough.*

The babble about localism and a separatist movement incites immediate disparagement from establishment leaders and property moguls, impatient as they are about this buzz, this pesky annoyance, this *noise*. Noise that tears them away from their ledgers of profit. Youthful energy – naive and idealistic though it may be – is sending a loud message to the leaders of the city. About income inequality and the lack of affordable housing.

About a growing underclass. About the hopelessness they feel when they try to imagine their future. *Stop complaining,* they're told. *We know what Hong Kong needs much better than you do. Go away and let us do our jobs. You – well, you should just listen to us because you are wrong, wrong, wrong.* Can you blame the young for ignoring such rebuffs? Seriously, how can they not? It's like my tiresome lover, who incessantly nags and berates me, saying the same things over and over and over again – *you cannot leave me, you are nothing without me.* What he fails to recognise is that I have been leaving him for years. I am leaving, am continuing to leave, will one day leave. Forever.

A spate of recent suicides among the young has brought those sad figures to an all-time statistical high. In answer, the education minister shells out HK$5000 per school to provide messages of hope. The city loudly proclaims how well the young are cared for, but something is clearly amiss. It has turned into an ongoing soap opera, M.A.S.H.[23] perhaps, where emotional brutality simmers and erupts in verbal and physical violence, baffling a hopelessly helpless leadership, terrifying the citizenry. The refrain of its theme song by Johnny Mandel, that opens with the notion of suicide as painless, was a sadly appropriate anthem for my chaotic city

---

23 The 1970 Robert Altman film needs no introduction, but it is the long-running TV series that resembles HK in recent times. M.A.S.H. refers to the 4077th Mobile Army Surgical Hospital in South Korea that was the setting for the black comedy.

in 2016, where we were confronted with, at best, a take it or leave it attitude.

Dear HK, enough! Your repetitive pleas will not change my mind. We need a new lens, with neither rose-coloured tints nor the smoggy blur of disappearance.

Dear HK, I'm breaking things off. May fortune always shine upon you.

(5)

Who could resist the lure of China? In 1991, after nine years of not setting foot in Hong Kong, I returned to visit my parents, and, for the first time, Mainland China.

During the years away, I had kept up Mandarin Chinese classes in the US. In 1991, I had not yet conceded failure, but complete literacy would always elude me. The one and only Chinese novel I managed to read in its original language was Eileen Chang's *The Golden Cangue*. It was a laborious effort, and in the end unsatisfying. As a comparative endeavour, I read the Alexandre Dumas novel *La Dame Aux Camélias* in its original French; my French literacy, I discovered, was more or less on par with my Chinese, but the French-English dictionary was easier to use than the

Chinese-English one. Eventually, when I broke down and read the English translations, the full power of both books was finally revealed to me.

But it was exciting to cross the border into the mainland that first time, to Guangzhou and Guilin, and to converse in passable Mandarin (Putonghua was not yet a word bandied around as frequently in global English). I got food poisoning on the Li River from eating its shrimp, but the next night in Yangshuo, seated in a cramped, makeshift restaurant and toasting with a Mao lookalike over a spicy clay pot meal, the illness was forgotten, merely a temporary inconvenience during this foray into my primary country of origin. Familiar as China felt, this border-crossing also confirmed my suspicions: China was a decidedly *foreign* country.

What I was less prepared for was how foreign Hong Kong had become. The grand march of history had transformed my city, and 1997 was now a looming reality. The city was prosperous but clean, both physically and spiritually, as the ICAC had virtually eradicated corruption. Although the handover felt alarmingly near, giving foreign journalists pause, the local populace mostly shrugged and said, *No big deal, it's just the way things are.* Although the Union Jack still flew, we were no longer a 'colony', having been a British dependent territory for a decade. The dependency was, however, less evident, as many of the top government and business positions were now occupied by a Chinese elite instead of British one, though they all still spoke (or tried to speak) the Queen's English.

Also, a notable population of young Hong Kong Chinese had returned from their 'immigration prisons' in Canada, Australia and elsewhere, armed with foreign passports, bodies, accents, attitudes and manners, some with friends, lovers and spouses from a rainbow of races. Filipinos had become the fastest growing Asian group, domestic helpers who camped in Central on their Sundays off, a practice that was still cause for anger among many HK Chinese. That changed as more and more Hong Kongers surrendered control of their lives and chores – cooking, cleaning and caring for their young and elderly, even tutoring their offspring in English – to Filipino helpers whose English was superior, even if not Queen's. In addition to the Filipinos, Russians, Nigerians and people of other nationalities had begun to occupy Chungking Mansion, new faces of globalised trade. Other Asians had also invaded the professions, as well as hyphenated Asians from the West. In my absence, the large new Kowloon Mosque had sprung up, a dominant sight in Tsim Sha Tsui, funded by compensation from the MTR after the subway's construction had damaged the old mosque. Similarly, Putonghua could more frequently be heard in the streets of the city.

A new cosmopolitanism had erupted in HK.

The eruption was most evident in nightlife. Lan Kwai Fong was a nightly party scene, right in the middle of the Central business district, where HK Chinese, expatriate residents and visitors alike all flocked. There were several jazz venues around town, and well-known musicians came from around the world to perform. Now we were not just a premier Chinese restaurant city but an international one. Now *everyone* ate sushi, antipasto, vindaloo, kimchi, moussaka, gỏicuốn, medium-rare steaks, tom yum gong, shucked raw oysters *et al*. Or so it seemed if you gazed at the surface of things, where the global gaze tends to alight.

Everyone in my world said, *Come home, come home, there are plenty of jobs, the economy's great!* During my visit, I ended up with four interviews for well-paid positions, even though I wasn't looking.

But New York was still home where I was The Writer, hacking out a living at the P.R. and marketing department of a large Wall Street law firm. New York was still The City for a writer like me and my then-husband, a jazz guitarist. We had a car, a home, a mortgage and a tenant in our two-family home on a tree-lined street in Brooklyn. I had by then published several stories in decent journals and been shortlisted for a couple of literary prizes. One story had been selected for an Asian-American women's fiction collection, *Home To Stay,* an anthology that was garnering critical attention. Plus I'd recently won a prestigious fiction fellowship from New York state, and was still floating on the euphoria of recognition. My life in the city meant hanging out with writers and artists, meeting editors who were interested in my work, giving readings in the Village and elsewhere to audiences who liked what they heard. My career as a writer felt like it was finally starting to take off.

But New York was still reeling from Black Monday, the October day in '87 when the stock market crashed and the promised Reaganomics trickle-down only flowed upstream, defying gravity. The US was on the cusp of the nineties, a decade that proved a financial seesaw. By then I had lived through a business career evolution worthy of a creationist's narrative. I had: been merged and acquired out of one job; scrambled through a period of unemployment; toyed as a researcher for a venture capitalist on a quest for dying brands; managed a nightly art production shift as a 'full-time freelancer' for a creative solutions new technology start-up; and made the final round of interviews for a management position at a GE subsidiary (they wanted the candidate to relocate to Princeton, New Jersey, to which the other applicant agreed and I did not). Meanwhile, layoffs were happening at the law firm and my boss warned we might be next. And New York was filthy, the crime rate was high and the economy was tanking like a lead balloon.

Plus my parents were growing older, alone in Hong Kong, without any of their children by their side.

Meanwhile, China was calling, with its grand promise of a better tomorrow. In step with an earlier generation of *wah kiu* who fell for that 愛國[24] lure just before the Cultural Revolution, I, too, chose to return (*temporarily*, I promised my husband; *I'll believe it when I see it,* he replied) to this China with Western characteristics. For the love of family, for a lust for life if not art, aided and abetted by the lure of 'home' and lovely lucre.

My second return to the city of my birth was life-changing, although HK blindsided me at first. Federal Express offered me a marketing manager position at their Hong Kong and China operation for over one and a half times my salary at the law firm, plus relocation costs. My boss, based in Hawaii, told me I had to learn this intranet 'email thing' the company used. I said yes, we rented out our home to good tenants and packed up our life for this grand adventure.

The first problem was housing. I was not an expatriate hire because of my local status, but I had been assured by my mother that I could easily find a rental for

---

24 愛國 (*aiguo*), or, literally, 'love the nation', was the siren revolutionary call to help rebuild China that so many overseas Chinese, especially those from Southeast Asia, heeded. The Cultural Revolution was not quite what most had in mind, but the shock of that did not diminish their love and patriotism, my uncle being one example despite the resultant loss of his Indonesian passport and lack of access to a new one when he arrived in Hong Kong. He remained stateless till he died, but remained proud of being Chinese and seemed not to regret his foray into the pig farm, where he was relegated in the name of being a good Chinese citizen who loved and served his nation.

far less than half my salary (true), and that second-hand cars, a necessity for my husband the musician, were not terribly expensive (also true). We always believe what we wish to believe, don't we? For love? The first place my husband and I saw in Sheung Shui we walked out of in less than a minute. I had not counted on how American I had become, and the standard of living to which I was accustomed. There was simply no way I could really live like a local. We eventually found a place that was slightly less than half my salary, a tiny furnished studio in Causeway Bay that overlooked the harbour for HK$23 000 a month. It seemed outrageous when my larger one-bedroom had only cost HK$150 000 to purchase a mere fifteen years earlier. But the location was convenient, my American husband could learn his way around the city more easily in this urban centre, and the flat had a decent-sized bathroom suited to our 'American' tastes. We dumped our over-large shipment of household effects into storage and accepted our reduced reality. By the time we realised our relatively inexpensive car would cost us HK$4000 a month to park, we simply grinned and bore it.

The second problem was my being a 'local' manager hired from the US. The staff considered me a *gwaipo* until they heard me speak Cantonese. The real problem was that I spoke English like an American with no HK accent, and could joke and drink and rabbit on about baseball,

Saturday Night Live, Hill Street Blues, Tennessee and other things American with the expatriate staff.

Digress with me a moment. In 1992, when I returned to this still-British city, the American population outnumbered the British. The North American accent was prized by locals as much if not more than Queen's English or the Received Pronunciation (RP) accent, and a surprising number of young North Americans spoke fluent Mandarin. A sizable number also spoke good Cantonese. More significantly, the democracy of a globalised younger generation had shifted, though not eradicated, the boundaries between 'them' (*gwai*) and 'us' (HK Chinese).

At Federal Express, an American management style prevailed. Now I was no longer one of the few local employees who addressed bosses by their first name instead of 'Mr'; now everyone used first names. Speaking English with an HK Chinese accent was not scorned but respected, this second language mastery being something most Americans could not emulate. Although the company established itself in Asia with an expatriate management team from the US, the goal was to get rid of these too-expensive expatriates. Notably, their salaries were not higher than those of local management, although they did get housing. There was still a divide, but it was not nearly as pronounced as it had been under the British colonial-style management at the airline in the seventies, where servitude, not initiative, was rewarded.

An Aristotelian reversal of fortunes indeed!

My real problem, however, was acceptance by the *local,* not the expatriate, staff. The first test was karaoke. Canto pop. Mando pop. Any pop. I could not say no to the other local managers, even though I didn't know a single Canto or Mando pop song. I still don't, and even my knowledge of Western pop is remarkably dated. But I was confident I could out-drink most HK Chinese, which gave me some advantage. By now I could also read Chinese well enough to get through most of the lyrics and fudge the rest. Pop music of any kind is fairly predictable, rather like genre fiction. Hear the basic structure and you too can sing Canto and even Mando pop passably well. Thus, I survived and was no longer considered quite as much of a she-devil.

Once I settled back into life with HK, I resumed Mandarin classes. Surely, I thought, my language skills would improve by leaps and bounds in a Chinese world, compared to in New York, where I never used Chinese except in class or Chinatown. My tutor was a former opera singer from Beijing who rolled his 'r's perfectly. He was a *dramatis personae* who had never left the stage and would zestfully intone my Chinese name, saying it a beautiful one of which I should be proud. Meanwhile, his wife collected fees with alacrity. *Ni ting wo shuo,* he would begin each lesson, *listen to me speak.* And then I would have to imitate the sentences until he was satisfied with my pronunciation.

More importantly, I could speak to my father, uncles and aunts in Mandarin, all those proud-to-be-Chinese folks from Indonesia. In particular, the uncle who had answered the *aiguo* call and left Indonesia for China was especially pleased.

Yet the longer I hung with HK, the worse my Mandarin became. The problem was all his Cantonese, seeping back into my consciousness, twisting my tongue, confusing my precarious literacy, assailing my loyalties. For the first time in my life, I truly appreciated how challenging HK's language and culture must have been for my parents when they arrived in the forties. Mum persevered, even though it was much harder for her, given her lack of Chinese literacy. But Dad got angry. The Chinese he so proudly mastered as a child in Indonesia, good enough to attend university in Shanghai, was mocked in this British-Canto colony. His Cantonese was unacceptably tainted with that 'nation's language' accent. It was probably why, with rare exceptions, he refused to spend his hard-earned cash in Cantonese restaurants, and took our family to eat Shantung, Chiu Chow and Peking cuisine instead, preferring these outsider Chinese worlds where he could speak Mandarin or accented Cantonese and sound like everyone else. In the end, it was English that gave my parents and family 地位, what Mum called 'position' but what was really an asocial ledge upon which we could perch, however precariously, in this class-and-status-conscious society – a society that excludes, or is at least not as kind as it could be, to those who cannot easily conform to its language.

For a brief time in my strange existence, I managed to sound almost like a Beijinger. On business trips up north, I was even praised for my 'excellent' Chinese. This was the nineties though, when Hong Kong and the mainland were on friendlier terms, when it was one country of two citizenries who were still interested in and even respected each other's differences, despite Tiananmen. By the mid 2000s, no matter how hard I tried to pronounce Putonghua, Beijingers of various stripes would heap scorn on my efforts as I was so obviously one of those uncouth southern 'savages', those running hounds of the West.

As for HK, all he did was flounce around saying, *That's just the way things are, stop making such a fuss. Just accept it.*

In 1994, three things happened in Hong Kong. Wong Kar-wai released *Chungking Express*, a film that would put HK on the world's cultural map in a new, unexpected, artier if fuzzier fashion; Planet Hollywood opened on Canton Road in Tsim Sha Tsui and the launch party in May closed down the area for a night as Jackie Chan and a host of other Hollywood and HK stars swanned down the concrete red carpet; and my first book, a novel-in-stories titled *Chinese Walls,* was released by a Hong Kong-based English-language publisher[25] of Asian writing, which set me on an alternate trajectory of a literary career, not the one I envisioned in New York City at the centre of English language publishing. It was not something I had ever imagined as a possibility.

This was in concert with HK's new and improved cosmopolitanism, a term that has multiple layers of meanings, and one that would be transformed, cogently and memorably, by the Ghanaian-British-American philosopher Kwame Anthony Appiah a little over a decade later.[26] Appiah is 101 days younger than I am, a random fact that connects me to this stranger. Reassuring, this same-generation echo of another's mind that converges with your own. As I mourn, after a fashion, in this elegy for HK, I may find comfort in memory, which is sometimes prickly, pernicious and perilous to one's well-being. How can it not

---

25 Asia 2000, the publisher, was the brainchild of an American journalist-turned-cultural/educational entrepreneur, Mike Morrow, who was fluent in Mandarin. The imprint struggled to be profitable and is now more or less dormant, the sad fate of more than one of my HK-based publishers. Which just goes to prove that a literary life in these here Asiatic parts can be precarious, perilous and not exactly the path to profit.

26 *Cosmopolitanism: Ethics in a World of Strangers,* W.W. Norton, 2006. An excerpt titled 'The Case for Contamination' appeared the in *The New York Times,* 1 January 2006. His earlier book, *The Ethics of Identity* (Princeton University Press, 2005), although more academic and harder for the lay reader, was what originally captivated me and made me a fan of his thinking.

be, all this remembering of an HK past, especially when you suspect that what's done is done, what's past is history and forgettable in this city of pernicious amnesia?[27]

But let's stay in the past for just a moment longer. HK being HK can only begrudgingly allow any joy for me, even the smallest amount (which is why he's such a difficult lover – let's be blunt, he's a pain, royally). A first book should be a thing of joy for any writer, as it was for me, although that joy was short-lived despite the good reviews, the attention of agents and publishers in New York, even the rapidity with which the first printing sold out. The novel was published under my then-byline, my English married name, Chako, a fictional albeit legal one, cobbled out of the first syllables of both my husband's and my last names. We each had an unusually convo-luted personal history with surnames, which led to the decision to create a new, joint name, one that could be construed as a gesture to feminism or sheer bloody mind-edness, depending on your perspective of what passes for marriage. For me it was a compromise for marital peace, coupled with a desire to create an American identity, because it was with this name that I pledged allegiance into citizenship in New York. In the US, it had been a

---

27 *Pernicious anaemia*, unlike HK's pernicious amnesia, is a real disease, a chronic illness caused by the body's impaired absorption of Vitamin B12, thus causing a low red blood cell count. It is also the cause of 80 per cent of megalobastic anaemia, according to one medical source. There is even a Pernicious Anaemia Society, one that would be delighted to accept your donations to help them help you. Now, if only the same attention could be paid to pernicious amnesia, HK and other megalopolises of the twenty-first century might have hope of recovering all those lost memories before time passes and, *well whaddya know*, it's already the twenty-second century.

comfortable enough name, vaguely exotic but pronounce-able, an invented reality to complement the fiction writer version of myself. Editors and readers never considered it a problem. Most of my fiction had been published under this name, and even my parents had accepted it as yet another ridiculous-but-not-pernicious decision of their her-way-or-the-byway eldest child.

So HK, in his inimitable way of juggling monkey wrenches, served up the problem of Kerala. My name, it appeared, was remarkably close to a Keralan surname, as one reader wrote to tell me, an inquiry rooted in his own desire to discover some familial connection (I've long suspected he was also an aspiring author, but have no definitive proof). More profoundly, the buzz in this town was: *How* dare *an Indian write about a Chinese family in HK, how* dare *she?* It did not matter that this was fiction, or that names do not always equate to race. This was HK, and this was the way things had to be.

In the non-existent literary world of HK at that time, one that could not imagine a world beyond its front door, there was an even more bizarre incident. Prior to publication, my editor surmised – correctly, as it turns out – that HK would read my novel as autobiography.[28]

---

28 The title Chinese Walls was vaguely autobiographical, I suppose, insofar as I learned it at the Wall Street law firm where I worked. When a law firm represents two clients on opposite sides of a deal, an invisible 'Chinese wall' goes up between the two teams working on that deal, and no conversations, papers or other information may be exchanged between members of the teams. However, if two young lawyers (or investment bankers, since the term applies equally to them) happen one night to fall in love or lust after one drink too many, the wall is neither Chinese nor a barrier, is it?

He even asked me to add a preface explaining that it was fiction. I contemplated this outrageous request, mostly because it was my first book and I did not want to risk the publisher's wrath with an uncooperative stance, going so far as to draft an afterword rather than a preface. In the end, though, I appealed to the publisher not to include this, as a novel should stand on its own. While I won that particular battle, it is only in retrospect that I understand how right the editor had been about the reading public.

While I was doing press for the book, a journalist, a young HK Chinese woman from a local English-language media outlet, interviewed me for a feature story. She was strangely insistent about the central American male character,[29] questioning me about him as if he were a real person until I finally said, *It is fiction, you know?* This did not deter her. She continued to speak about him as if he were real, drawing connections to my own life in Brooklyn, which was clearly how I must have met the man. The only conclusion I could draw was that she had fallen in love with him, which readers sometimes do with my fictional characters,[30] as even I have done from time

---

29   Vince da Luca, originally from Brooklyn, New York, who grew up in a home on a street I once lived on and who bears a curious resemblance to several American and Chinese men I knew or had known at the time of his creation. How could he not? He had to come from somewhere. But of all the Vinces or Vincents I've ever known, this Vince is nothing like any of them because no novelist in her right mind would be stupid enough to name her characters after real people who exhibit the same traits, unless it's deliberately done to make some kind of perverse point.

30   Some readers, I would later learn, even fall in lust with my characters. The reader who told me this was unusually open about it all. It startled me until I considered that his father had been a literature professor and that he himself also consumed literature voraciously. I wish I had thought to ask him if there were a way to create a virtual reality out of my fictional characters to distribute to all those lonely hearts in need of lust, love or merely companionship for a night or two. It would have been one way to increase book sales.

to time with characters in literature. However, she might have lacked sufficient experience of reading literature to understand this psychological transference, just as she proved too inexperienced a journalist to write such a feature, because I ended up virtually dictating the entire story to her, which she laboriously wrote down almost word for word. I watched her do this, stunned. It was a long and slow interview but resulted in a flattering piece about my book since the author will hardly speak disparagingly about her own work.

This experience was such a reminder of dictation at school when I was child. Each week, the teacher would assign an English passage for us to study or a Chinese passage for us to memorise. The dictation assignment in English was to reproduce exactly what the teacher read, and in Chinese class to reproduce the piece from memory.

My Chinese teacher had an easy time marking my dictation, because I had been unable to comprehend the assignment, given orally a few days earlier, to memorise the piece. As a result, I showed up to class unprepared, and turned in a blank notebook for which I received a big, fat zero. The teacher was nice though, taking me aside to re-explain the assignment, slowly, for what she must have considered a somewhat slow child as opposed to one who simply did not really understand Cantonese when it was properly, not colloquially, spoken. It was a life-changing moment for me at six, to know that the sounds you heard did not equate to what you thought you heard, no matter how hard you paid attention. In the makeup assignment, I got a 100 because rote memorisation of what was printed in a book was easy compared to comprehending spoken Cantonese. Which is probably why even Cantonese fails us in HK, the same way English does, because the teacher must set aside time for non-native speakers who, by all rights, should not be in a classroom learning Chinese alongside native speakers. Unfortunately, to this day, the HK Education Department hasn't really worked out how to handle this inconvenient reality of our city's population.

That journalist, I decided, might have thought 'writing' equalled 'dictation'. Her education had been at one of HK's elite English medium schools,[31] a fact she confirmed when, in my stunned state, I inquired, as diplomatically as possible, where she had gone to school. She may have done university abroad, but this is a hunch rather than a fact.

In fairness to HK, several features by other local journalists about my first and later books proved less stunningly strange, and the little joy of being interviewed

31 She attended a rival girls school, neither Maryknoll nor New Method, which I attended. Whether or not I should name the school gives me pause. After all, there is no reason to cast aspersions on a local institution, one that is famous for its high English- and literature-teaching standards, on the basis of one graduate. She might have been a science student, or simply from a rich family who could afford to buy her the requisite education, college degree and respectable job, a student who perhaps had not had the pleasure of studying literature but had good enough English to 'slum it' for a time as a sort of journalist before marrying the right HK boy to relieve her of having to work.

well by competent writers lingers, long after the local media coverage is forgotten and the newsprint recycled at markets for wrapping fish and other delicacies.

But, Kerala. Kerala, by way of HK's intransigence, was how I became Xu Xi.

I have occasionally told this story, and continue to tell new and improved versions of this real-but-not-real authorial name, which some call a pen name. When the Keralan crisis erupted over my first book, the publisher looked at my Chinese name[32] and asked if I would consider using it as a byline. The full name is a clunky mouthful for anyone who doesn't know pinyin, which many HK Chinese do not, nor can you reasonably expect English-language readers in Asia or elsewhere to be familiar with a language of transliteration, even if China believes the world ought to know it. But these are not real considerations in art or life. My shortened Chinese name was graphically pleasing, a thing of beauty. It also meant I could now sign my name with the illiterate's X, something any writer must occasionally desire – being illiterate, I mean. Which is why the first edition of my

---

32 許素細. HK Cantonese speakers who read it aloud will invariably frown, look puzzled and more often than not ask why the last character isn't something else. Some even suggest both characters of the forename should be something entirely different. In fact, my Chinese name has been rendered in print by HK Chinese editors and others who never bothered to ask as three entirely different characters from the true version. It is odd, this presumption of what my Cantonese name ought to be, since, in the first instance, I am not Cantonese but Fujianese, and, more to the point, this was the Mandarin name my father chose to give me. Thank goodness for my opera singer Beijing tutor! After a lifetime of HK ignorance about my Cantonese name, my father was finally vindicated.

second book, *Daughters of Hui*, was bylined Xu Xi, with my English name in brackets beside it. The latter was the editor's suggestion, concerned as he was that no one would know who this author was. It was reasonable I think, since even I did not know who Xu Xi was, at least not yet, and even now I sometimes don't quite know who she is, except that she has been inside me for awhile now. When I teach my MFA students and the subject of pen names arises, my cautionary tale is to think about this *before* you publish your first literary work, and not seventeen years later[33] as I did.

A few years earlier in New York, I met an author who had similar problems due to genre and identity. She had been a romance writer who migrated into literary fiction, and we read together out of the Asian-American anthology of women writers that included our work. She is part Hawaiian but was given a generic American name at birth, under which she successfully published several romance novels. She has since gone on to publish literary work with significant Hawaiian connections under a moniker that represents her mixed race. Her first literary novel appeared the same year mine did, a

---

33 A short story, 'The Sea Islands', was my first literary publication as an adult, appearing in 1979 in the second issue of *Imprint*, a journal at the University of Hong Kong that published only four issues and then died. Which further proves the likely lack of profit in HK literary publishing, as no other successful commercial or academic endeavour in HK would so quickly disappear before it even had a second to breathe. That story was published under my Indonesian legal name. My birth name was a Chinese-Fukienese (or Fujianese) transliteration that my grandfather concocted; his inability to render the English language sensibly is about the equivalent of my inability to use Chinese sensibly. We are a complicated family. However, standard Fujianese transliteration is even more esoteric than pinyin, and back when Grandpop came up with our original English surname in Indonesia, pinyin was still a movement of the future.

not-so-random coincidence about being the kind of writers we are – transcultural, transnational, complicated – but, as my late MFA thesis director used to say about the drafts of my early novels which he found too simplistic: *Complications, my dear, you need to add complications*. He was Hungarian, that writer, a political exile in America who, like Nabokov, switched to English for his fiction. I dedicated my second book to him and sent him a copy, but he had died a few years earlier, as his wife wrote to tell me when it arrived.

I am less grateful to HK than I should be for launching my literary career. My agent in New York warned me against surrendering world rights to a 'foreign' publisher, but I did so for this three-book deal, something I would later come to regret. HK is ambitious but insular; international book distribution is even more difficult than publishing, because profits are razor-thin unless you happen to publish a best-selling Chinese author in translation who wins a major international prize. It was difficult, if not impossible, to get attention for a serious English-language novel published in Hong Kong or Asia. Yet blink, and twenty or so years later, Amazon, print-on-demand, E-books and other devices, coupled with the dying power of copyright thanks to Google,[34] have

---

34 In 2015, the US Second Circuit court sided with Google in *Authors Guild v. Google*, a lawsuit that lasted over a decade and which I followed with interest, being a long-time member of the Authors Guild. A few years earlier, one of my publishers told me that

113

completely transformed what it means to be an author in Asia. HK was truly post-modern and post-colonial before its time, and twenty-first century HK sometimes gives that notion credence. To be a writer now in HK is no more or less difficult than being a virtual parakeet who publishes a book. This might be good for birds, and means we humans can stop being merely human and adopt personae as animals, vegetables or minerals, as a book by a cauliflower will undoubtedly garner huge returns and millions of hits for its readings on YouTube – oh to be a cauliflower!

This second return to HK ended well, because in between, I spent a year or so in Singapore for Federal Express, where tropical rainfall and birds of paradise offered a rare respite from HK. HK fumed and pouted but I ignored him, instead entertaining myself with my husband's keyboard for hours, learning to play 'La Vie en Rose' in concert with the rhythm of its original French lyrics. You need to learn a few clichés from time to time, because the more you examine the origins of things, the more you understand that HK is not that

much of my earlier work was in Google Books, something I hadn't known, as it wastes too much time and effort to google yourself regularly just to find out who's reading, writing about or possibly stealing your work. It is enough that *someone, anyone* reads my work, and HK in particular has blessed me with an assiduous library acquisition program, as most of the public libraries have my books, something I also did not know until some time in the nineties when my late Toronto-based aunt, a Chinese-language author, told me they were. She had gone to the library when she was in town to see if her book (a collection of essays about overseas Chinese life that she published as a regular column in the *Ming Pao* 明報) was in the library, and she taught me to do likewise, even taking me to the library at City Hall to show me. I have been lucky with aunts, as another aunt I grew up around was an Indonesian storyteller.

different from any other complicated lover, being part frog and part prince. Frogs you either kiss or dismiss, unless it's Kermit singing 'The Rainbow Connection', in which case you'd rather be a pig (although Miss Piggy is about as ungrateful to Kermit as I am to HK). We're like that, we objects of affection and desire. We can't help being selfish divas when the opportunity presents itself, because we all like a little delusion in life. Besides, it's hard to forget that being any kind of diva was once upon a time about as impossible as being a frog. But it's good to grow up and forget. *Fade far away, dissolve and quite forget / What thou amongst the leaves has never known.*

Keats knew: it's better to be a bird.

VI

Dear HK,
再見 is the wrong goodbye.

Here I am, already saying goodbye before the end. A good ending, as any fiction writer knows, is preceded by all kinds of obstacles to desire and joy. The end to this HK story is no exception. My aunt, my *yee ma*, died of liver cancer shortly after I returned to HK. It was difficult, that death, painful and prolonged; she and her lifelong companion, my storyteller aunt, never got to live together in the retirement home they built in Bandung. Helping to clean out their Hong Kong home, I was glad I had returned because at least I got to see her before she died. Later, I left my job in Singapore and returned to Hong Kong. My husband and I divorced, ending a twelve-year marriage. A year later, I joined *The Asian Wall Street Journal* as their circulation director. This paper route job was peculiarly timed because there I was, distributing newspapers around the region just when newsprint was dying. The year 1997 and the handover arrived, and my third book, *Hong Kong Rose,* was published that year. It sold out immediately and then disappeared, along with my publisher.

Meanwhile, I'd fallen in love with a man from New Jersey. In 1998, I packed up my corporate life (forever, I said and still say) and moved into his New York City home. My aunt's death had left me and my siblings with an unexpected inheritance. Even though it was not huge, it was enough to fuel my courage to leave HK and embrace the writing life full time. Death of an intimate changes things when you least expect it.

It would be twelve years before I would return again to live in HK, although I spent almost as much time with HK as I did hanging out in New York, and also New Zealand. I purchased a small, inexpensive home on the South Island in 2003, in which to perch for a month or so at a time and write. However, I lived mostly with my man in New York – or at least, New York was always where I went to 'go home', and where the majority of my stuff was parked.

The long goodbye is a feature of my man's family, a running joke they and their spouses perpetuate each time the family gathers. By now I am almost a spouse, since we're well into our nineteenth year as a couple. Recently, at a reading I gave in New York, his niece introduced me as her aunt to another audience member. It was a pleasurable moment, as I like being an aunt, or grandaunt, as I've become thanks to my nephew in France who is now a dad. 'Aunt' is a role that suits me. I once told my man he would fare better if we didn't get married, as I tend to leave husbands, but that is just cowardice of a different stripe. Never mind, HK ignores everything I tell him about this man in my life, because all he knows, sees and cares about is being HK, the lover who won't let go. The three monkeys could be his mascot.

It is late spring, 2016, and the city is alternately overcast, rainy, with the occasional respite of sun rays. The cruellest month is over, which is always a relief, although this year's was less cruel, as winter kept me very, very warm in the Arizona desert. Yet now, back with HK, I find he will not let go, insists on holding on, in much the same way my 96-year-old mother lives on, in generally good health, although she no longer knows who she or anyone else is. There are moments we – meaning the two nurses and helper we've employed to care for her at home – think Mum does know the state of her existence, and exclaims at *the horror, the horror* of it all. We do not know for sure, as the Alzheimer's mind is not easily knowable.

It is late spring in 2016, past that cruellest month,

and T.S. Eliot continues to worry me, as he has for so long now it's almost like DNA.

> *What are the roots that clutch, what branches grow*
> *Out of this stony rubbish? Son of man,*
> *You cannot say, or guess, for you know only*
> *A heap of broken images, where the sun beats,*
> *And the dead tree gives no shelter, the cricket no relief,*
> *And the dry stone no sound of water.*

Last month, the engineer who is managing the construction of our new home told us there was water – good, soft water – in the well his team had dug on our rural New York property. It was a little joy, knowing water in our future home will not be hard, as it is in our current home on the lot next door. That water could be as soft as in our New York City home and my Hong Kong home, the bedsit on my mother's rooftop.

Sometime soon, in the next month or so, the movers will pack up my office at the university in Hong Kong, followed by my life on this rooftop, and ship all these personal effects to New York. The rooftop will still be my part-time home for the foreseeable future. We, meaning my siblings and I, are returning it to its original state, a guest room designed by Dad to ape a Japanese hotel room, with an exceptionally large, if ancient, bathroom. We return 'home' somehow, whether to a hotel-room-studio-flat in Causeway Bay, or to actual hotel rooms where I've spent so many nights of my adult existence. An American who frequents my Kowloon hotel bar once told me he had earlier lived for several years in that same hotel. *What was it like?* I wanted to know. *Wonderful,* he replied, smiling, the memory a comfort against the exigencies of life in this city. It reminded me of early life in Singapore, where I once resided in a hotel suite for over a month. Later, I returned to Hong Kong and lived briefly at a hotel in Causeway Bay, a hotel that no longer exists because a new group has taken over those premises. Homes are like that. They vanish from your life but not your memory. *Wonderful.*

But I was saying goodbye to my lover.

If you are a squirrel, there are apparently nine ways to say goodbye in simplified Chinese. A 2013 blog post by a squirrel, these virtual animals who are becoming virtual writers with alarming alacrity, suggests that *zaijian* or 再見 (in traditional Chinese characters) is the 'most vanilla goodbye' that you learn in 'your first day of Chinese class'. Actually, what I learned was 人爸爸媽媽手腳牙花草瓜米茶牛鳥 . . . etc., but I was three or four and already supposed to know Chinese. My number two sister and I can still recite these opening pages of vocabulary in our kindergarten primer. I can almost picture the colourful images accompanying those words – human being, father, mother, hand, foot, teeth, flower, grass, melon, rice, tea, cow, bird . . . the essential Cantonese words we recited to each other and never forgot. Squirrels, however, would probably prefer to learn the character for 'nut', which is far too difficult if you're three or four and just beginning to learn to read the language. Our primer did not include 'nut'.

HK is not amused. *Stop digressing*, he says, irritated by my attempts at play. How do you tell such a *see-rye-ous*[35] one that life need not always be serious? The problem is that things are dire and terribly serious these days in the city. Roofs at major universities collapse, as do the walls of historic structures we wish to preserve. Meanwhile the politicos bicker over the correct way to speak to sovereign leaders.[36] It will be so much easier when HK has its own guide to all the forms of proper address and discourse with the various party leaders who will undoubtedly continue to visit us from time to time.

There's no telling a petulant HK anything, though. Sometimes I wonder what kept me with him for so long.

---

35 Credit for this linguistic invention goes to Jenny Wai.

36 In May of 2016, Zhang Dejiang, chairman of the National People's Congress, visited Hong Kong for three days. It was a grand affair, and the government cordoned off his travel path through the city with enough police presence to make us wonder if, in fact, we had accidentally become a police state while no one was watching. Zhang met with four of the Pan Democrats, opponents of the current CE who were vocal in their displeasure, seizing this opportunity to 'speak to Beijing', something so rarely granted to them given their non-conformist views (with respect to the established order of things as dictated by the Hierarchy of Power, that is). However, Joshua Wong, a student leader of the Umbrella Movement, loudly criticized the Pan Democrats for daring to suggest to Zhang that the current CE CY Leung should be replaced, because it wasn't Zhang's role to make such a decision for HK! Even the politicos who normally agree are bickering. HK doesn't agree with itself about much of anything these days, least of all how to chart our future.

Habit, perhaps, the comfort of the familiar. But you can prolong a love affair past its use-by date and then there you are, *stuck in the middle*[37] with HK, which is not an ideal place to be.

Instead I will use Goodbye No. 9, the one deemed most formal and polite according to the squirrel, 失陪了, or *shipei le*, because it is an apology, expressing my regrets that I can no longer accompany HK, uttered as politely as possible to this not-so-polite lover, this angry younger man, this tenacious spirit that will not be broken by mere words.

37 'Stuck in the Middle', as the song was originally titled, is by Joe Egan and Gerry Rafferty, and was released by their band Stealers Wheel in 1972. This Scottish folk/rock band achieved a brief flash of fame, but the original band members left and others reformed it, as bands do. After 1975, Stealers Wheel disbanded entirely and their music faded from global consciousness for a time until Quentin Tarantino alighted upon the song and featured it in his 1992 debut film *Reservoir Dogs*. Which just goes to show that if you wait long enough, history will find a way of repeating itself.

(6)

And so, in 2010, I returned to HK's side to live with him for the last time.

Does my story really need a beginning, middle and end? That is what we teach fiction writers, but this prolonged elegy is a different animal entirely. Certainly not a squirrel and its obsession with nuts; rather more a snake, a sinuous and lazy one that won't move from its sunny perch unless disturbed or hungry. Snakes are efficient, pythons especially, as they will gorge on a gigantic meal and then rest for a long, long time. I am a snake, according to the Chinese lunar astrological calendar, and I am comfortable in that skin.

2010 is a long way from 1998, when I last left Hong Kong – twelve years to be exact, an entire lunar cycle of animals. Another sudden death – Dad's – shortly after I departed. Then Mum's Alzheimer's erupted. The fates somersaulted and sent me back to the city, eventually. I had been inhabiting the flight path connecting New York, Hong Kong and the South Island of New Zealand, and it was exhausting. Above all, it became clear that *someone* had to live with Mum. In 2010, I said, *Here I am*.

The problem with not getting married, unlike my three younger siblings who succumbed to the marital state, is that one's significant other is perhaps more tolerant than a husband of a long-distance relationship. Yet this, too, has brought challenges. 'Modern Love' is the name of a column that appears regularly in the *New York Times*. Every kind of 'love', from the romantically delusional woman who stalked a friend of mine to the agony of loving a terminal intimate, as another friend did, appears in this column. Modern love is complicated, 複雜, a term that is even more complicated in Chinese, used as it is for anything too difficult to explain, tackle or resolve, much like the state of our city in these times. Umbrellas foster revolutions and filibustering passes for a political process. To be 複雜 is almost to deny resolution. Perhaps we are afraid of the possible outcome, and to deny . . . what is it we deny? Accountability? Fault? Responsibility? The government these days is good at denying all three.

Enough! exclaims HK. He says I am being unfair, that I was *supposed* to be allowing memory to speak, to narrate the story of my life during this last return to the city. This third and last of my HK eras is 2010 to the present day (and counting). By the middle of 2016, I will no longer be obligated by a contract for work. After that, my HK life will be for love of family, if not HK, and in time, my life in the city will come to its end, although it is probably unwise to predict exactly what shape that end will take.

Of this most recent return, however, 2013 proved a significant year.

The year began badly. On 5 January 2013, Leung Ping-kwan, or as he was better known by his pen name, Yesi 也斯, died, an immense loss to our local literary world. He wrote in Chinese, in Cantonese, capturing the face and soul of the city, and inspired many writers here. If we could have named a poet laureate, it would have been PK, as those of us who conversed in Cantolish called him. He had a capacious mind, and it was possible to talk to him about everything, as he determined anything observable, do-able and imaginable to be worth his consideration. HK and I, we mourned.

The year began with a list of resolutions on my fifty-ninth birthday in late January:

1.   Drink more water
2.   Drink less vodka
3.   Lose the muffin top

4. Exercise with greater discipline and regularity
5. Eat less
6. Move around more
7. Sleep more
8. Play less Angry Birds
9. Watch less TV (including the 24/7 news feeds)
10. Turn off email
11. Watch the market and invest more
12. Spend less
13. Save more
14. Write and read and write and read and write and read

Sometime in early February, I held up that imaginary mirror and said, *Take a good look at yourself and know who you are.* 2013 was a year that ended with a decision to work-to-rule. It was the first time in my life I ever entertained such an idea, having willingly done more than required for every job I ever held. Professional self-respect has always mattered to me, and that has nothing to do with money or pleasing the boss.

This serpentine year, the Chinese year of the snake, was the mid-point of two three-year employment contracts at the university that chained me to Hong Kong. It was also in this lunar year Mum fell and broke her hip, and of the operation, convalescence and recovery that changed her life, and mine.[38] That year, the head of the English department who had cajoled me into accepting my first (and likely last) full-time academic position to start up the MFA resigned, and for the next two and a half years (and counting), the department remained headless. It has been a little like hanging out in Sleepy Hollow, that legendary town along the highway north of my home in upstate New York. The town was home to the fictional Ichabod Crane, an over-sensitive, superstitious schoolmaster who dreams of leaving his job for a life of wealthy leisure by marrying the beautiful Katrina, the daughter of a wealthy farmer. But a headless horseman haunts the town and one night spooks him, sending him off in a fright, without his beloved Katrina, never to return. That year, the headless horseman of the English department spooked us mercilessly, a constant threat in the air. An ominous silence hung – you could only guess at what was next in store – yet nothing really changed, except little by little, the dignity of our profession was eroded, nothing moved forward, and, like in Sleepy Hollow, a strange stasis took hold.

In 1820, the New York writer Washington Irving published his ghostly tale 'The Legend of Sleepy Hollow', set around Tarrytown, so named because folks

---

38 Most elderly people, especially those with Alzheimer's, rapidly deteriorate after such a traumatic physical experience, but Mum soldiered on and today walks daily, with assistance.

tarried too long there, sometimes to their peril. The narrator's description of the place is reminiscent of my hanging out too long with HK and the university:

> I mention this peaceful spot with all possible laud; for it is in such little retired Dutch valleys, found here and there embosomed in the great State of New York, that population, manners, and customs, remain fixed; while the great torrent of migration and improvement, which is making such incessant changes in other parts of this restless country, sweeps by them unobserved. They are like those little nooks of still water which border a rapid stream; where we may see the straw and bubble riding quietly at anchor, or slowly revolving in their mimic harbor, undisturbed by the rush of the passing current. Though many years have elapsed since I trod the drowsy shades of Sleepy Hollow, yet I question whether I should not still find the same trees and the same families vegetating in its sheltered bosom.

2013 was also the year of ridding myself of all perches on my flight path. First, I sold my writing retreat, the South Island 'crib' in New Zealand. Later went the flat in Tsim Sha Tsui, originally purchased as a *pied-à-terre* for after my mother passed away and we no longer had a family home. A prolonged agony prevailed that year, as first this, then that and then everything else was divested from a future with HK, because that was the year I finally knew: it's time to leave the city for good.

Except that I couldn't.

For one thing, I still had three more years of my contract with the university, and even after the MFA program was unceremoniously closed in 2015, students in my care remained, students I would not abandon unless the university forced me to do so.

But the greatest significance of the year 2013 is that it marked my transformation into Professor Chaos.

On *South Park*, Comedy Central's late-night animated satirical series about outrageous and politically incorrect fourth graders at a Colorado school, Professor Chaos is the alter ego of Butters, a timorous child, the butt of jokes and victim of bullies. One night, in utter frustration at his beleaguered existence, Butters fashions a helmet and mask out of aluminium foil to complement his green and yellow costume, and *voilá*, a superhero is born. His first evil act as Professor Chaos – to flood the town – trickles down to nothingness, as the garden hose in his hand drips too slowly and eventually dries up. His sidekick, General Disarray, another boy superhero, can only watch in despair. Professor Chaos echoes that other quixotic character, the schoolteacher Ichabod Crane, whom Irving describes as 'an odd mixture of small shrewdness and simple credulity. His appetite for the marvellous, and his powers of digesting it, were equally extraordinary; and both had been increased by his residence in this spellbound region.'

That year, my writer-in-residence life became increasingly surreal, and it soon was apparent, after several vain attempts to address 'issues' expressed by the College[39] about the MFA program, that the university simply wanted to get rid of the program for reasons they could not fully articulate. Why else the numerous obstacles, some verging almost on the irrational, and the demands for more and more reports that no one appeared to read? We were a tiny program. By our fifth year we were even profitable, according to the university's financial model, one that made no allowance for the 'low-residency' cost efficiencies of the program. The

---

39 The 'College', headed by a dean and generally known as CLASS, is the College of Liberal Arts and Social Sciences. It is in CLASS where the Department of English is housed. Each semester, as program leader of the MFA, I was asked to provide justification for all its regular expenses, duplicating the exact same information submitted the prior semester. Questions about how the program ran would be asked repeatedly, and I would copy and paste the text from memos previously submitted, simply changing the date. Likewise, the voluminous reports I had to submit all year long, often with repeated requests for the exact same information previously submitted, could also be achieved, I realised, by copying and pasting. These curious requests came from CLASS, and at first I wondered if it was because the MFA was a new and unfamiliar program, thus causing anxiety for those who read the reports. It was, after all, the only low-residency degree offered at the university. However, I soon discovered that other programs experienced more or less the same thing. Pernicious amnesia apparently was a condition of CLASS. One colleague (since retired), a program leader with comparable reporting requirements, nicknamed CLASS 'Mordor' after the impenetrable fictional universe in JRR Tolkien's Lord of the Rings. In fairness to Mordor, the Finance Office, or FO, at the university exhibited similar behavioural tendencies to CLASS, which led me to conclude that hell and the hand basket had simply become my present reality, an unlucky hand dealt me by Lady Luck. Either that or I had taken a wrong turn off the highway and ended up in another of Irving's fictions with Rip Van Winkle, the man who falls asleep for twenty years after accidentally stumbling into a company of 'odd looking personages playing at ninepins' who, he surmises were 'evidently amusing themselves'. When Rip approaches them, however, they stopped playing and 'stared at him with such fixed statue-like gaze, and such strange, uncouth, lack-luster countenances, that his heart turned within him, and his knees smote together.' They more or less drug Rip with their liquor, which puts him into a long sleep. So perhaps I too was simply asleep, and this CLASS-FO prolonged agony was a nightmare from which I would eventually awake.

fact that the MFA contributed to raising the international ranking of the department, and garnered respect for its highly successful outcomes made absolutely no impact. Why, I wondered, did they even bother establishing this program in the first place?

My solace was being Professor Chaos.

One of my favourite movies is *Being John Malkovich*, a quirky, irrepressibly imaginative foray into a portal that is the mind of real-life actor Malkovich. The portal is accidentally discovered by Craig, an unemployed puppeteer who reluctantly takes a temp job as a filing clerk in a strange, Escher-esque building. My being Professor Chaos was somewhat but not exactly like that, since university life drove me to seek a portal to escape that dauntingly absurd world. I badly wanted to resign, but the wonderful students and faculty of the program I helped to create, as well as my department colleagues who also suffered in their own Sleepy Hollows – all these people who later spoke up for the MFA when the walls came tumbling down – I knew I couldn't just walk out. When life sucks, you either despair (and Craig's dance of despair and disillusionment in the Malkovich film is tragicomedy at its finest), or else you rise above that despair through imagination and writing and art.

Chaos and Disarray.

Fast forward to today and 2013 is already a memory.

Many of the players have moved on to their respective Acts II or V, as have I. Right now, today, a cardboard helmet and felt cape and shield – Professor Chaos's replicas, presented to me by my MFA students who protested the closure of their program – adorn my writer-in-residence office, along with a drawing of a bespectacled Asian female Chaos punching out a senior management figure at the university. Soon, the boxes will arrive for me to pack up my books and art and files, including the few items that have sat in my office since 2013 from my former New Zealand home. Those repetitive reports will go into the recycling bin, as will the hundreds of communiqués I no longer need to read.

But Chaos and Disarray will be lovingly packed up and shipped to my home in the US, a reminder of what endures, ameliorating the despair that HK has once again failed me, as he does, as he has, as long as he's been my lover. As the city probably always will.

VII

P.S.[40]

The little girl in green overalls and matching shirt holds
her Filipino helper's hand, their arms swinging in concert as they dash downhill together. They could almost
be sisters, the helper is so young, except that the girl is
distinctly Chinese and the woman, who might be eth-
nically Chinese, has blended into the darker features
and blood of the Philippines. Years later when the girl
remembers this 姊姊, big sister, she once loved *with all
her heart* and said so in English, constantly, much to her
mother's consternation, she will wonder where she is
now. Or perhaps hers is a family who kept in touch with
their domestic helper, as some do, the way a 妹仔 sister-
child of an earlier generation became family, indentured

40 In 1625, the English essayist Francis Bacon wrote on the subject of postscripts: 'I knew
    one, that when he wrote a Letter, he would put that which was most Materiall, in the
    Post-script, as if it had been a By-matter.'

133

– as those impoverished girls were – for life when purchased by a wealthy family to be their domestic slave.

All around me, money tries to buy love, or something like love.

I live in an upper middle-class neighbourhood, or at least this is what our hilltop home has become, a hilltop that was once the district for those with not quite enough money to purchase poorly constructed private flats for a pretence to respectability, as my mother so desperately desired in 1970. I was sixteen and detested this move away from Tsim Sha Tsui, away from the penthouse flat overlooking the harbour that was Dad's pride and joy. My father is dead, my mother not much longer for this world. I am almost but not quite eligible for my senior citizen MTR card. It no longer matters why I was born or whether or not my parents could have loved me better or more. Dad survived the bankruptcy that necessitated our move, and Mum has forgotten that she can never forgive her husband his excesses, along with everything else she has forgotten that once defined her existence. These days, however, the love I feel for my parents is no longer complicated by the more tiresome emotional aspects of love.

Instead, when memory speaks, what is left for me to puzzle over is whether or not money did buy my love.

Love is almost irrelevant when it comes to me and HK. At best it is sentimental – the stuff of gorgeous wedding photos at Hong Kong Gardens or City Hall, or posed against the false stages in Kowloon Tong's bridal salons. What the city demands, what it has always gotten from me, is a love that's inextricably bound to duty. HK money was always lucrative, more so than that of New York or other places, but this last return has felt too much like a deal with a devil I know, made to protect me from a devil I don't know, the one always just around the corner, looming, threatening. That is the problem of life with HK, this constant companion, this desperate love. Despite the money, desperation is not love, and these days, Hong Kong is too desperate, too panicked, too afraid of losing all that he was. Little by little, he is changing, must change, will change, whether he likes it or not.

Today, now, this city could probably learn a lesson from my mother's Alzheimer's. A little memory is a dangerous thing; forgetfulness can sometimes be sweeter.

It's 2016 and almost summer. A year from now, Hong Kong will have been a Special Administrative Region of China for twenty years, as long as my man in New York has been the man in my life. Surely that constancy, without HK's clinging demands, is sweeter? Or at least easier, less anguished, filled with laughter if you let it be.

I am loath to end this Dear John letter, perhaps because I know HK won't read it, will simply cast it aside, the way he does when something doesn't fit with his notions of what he wants, what he thinks is right, what he believes is his due. When did he become so sure of himself, so willing to self-destruct in the face of reality? When did he stop listening to his own heart, choosing instead to live so determinedly in a frenzied *now, now, now,* consuming every present moment with such gluttonous fervour? When did he stop hearing the voice of love, the one trying to tell him that he must first and foremost love himself, before demanding the love of others?

It isn't easy saying goodbye. Even though love affairs are perpetually ending, this one was supposed to be forever. When memory speaks, I am still gazing at the harbour, the one my mother saw in a dream and my father wanted to own because it signalled he had arrived, succeeded, become *somebody* in this city of luck and opportunity. The harbour lights are excessive now, a nightly extravaganza of wasted energy that the tourist board names 'a symphony of lights'. Visually raucous, impressive to behold. A face for the world that HK doesn't want to lose. *Lose it,* I say: life isn't only about face.

But as usual he doesn't hear me, just as he won't hear my final farewell.

Appendix

For the curious reader, I would like to suggest the following additional readings, online resources and anecdotes.

In the Time Before
The Umbrella Movement
http://www.scmp.com/topics/occupy-central

1
China's national anthem
义勇军进行曲: China's national anthem translates as 'March of the Volunteers'.

The Chordettes
Live performance of the tune 'Mr. Sandman' from 1958: https://www.youtube.com/watch?v=VNUgsbKisp8

II

Leung Ping-Kwan 也斯, 'we travel with lots of stuff '
   In: Leung Ping-Kwan, Amblings, trans., Kit Kelen et
   al., ASM, Macau, 2010.

Hong Kong Scouts further reading
   'Rainbow Merit Badge' by Brooke Allen, New York
   Times, 19 July 2012, as well as 'The Boy Scouts of
   America is "Reviewing" its Anti-Gay Discrimination'
   by Steve Williams, Care 2, 27 May 2015, and 'Boy
   Scout Files May Be Used in Sex Abuse Trial, Judge
   Rules' by Laila Kearney, Reuters, 10 January 2015,
   among other media coverage.

**The school on Nairn Road sporting a Chairman
   Mao portrait: Mong Kok Workers' Children
   School (since renamed: Workers' Children
   Secondary School)** A visit to the school by an
   Australian documentary television crew shortly prior
   to the riots in the sixties is detailed in Peter Moss's
   book *No Babylon: A Hong Kong Scrapbook* (IUniverse,
   New York/Lincoln/Shanghai, 2006). The visit ends
   badly after the crew is confronted by angry students.
   Outsiders, especially Westerners, were not welcome
   on the school's premises. Moss, who worked for the
   HK government at the time, is fascinated by the 'vitu-
   perative nature of the slogans covering these walls of

learning' and reflects on the incident as follows: *Why did they hate us so much?*

III

MFA program closure at City University of Hong Kong

For further information surrounding the debacle of the closure of this MFA program, please visit the Facebook site mounted by students and faculty around the theme 'Save CityU MFA' see https://www.facebook.com/SaveCityUMFA?fref=ts. The Tumblr site documents the extensive international media interest, see http://savecityumfa.tumblr.com/ and has links to much of the media coverage and letters of protest sent to the university by students, faculty and supporters from around the world.

HK as a space for writers

'One better does it with the understanding that this place does not believe in "architects of the souls", as the old socialist phrase goes, that it doesn't provide much space for artistic development.' — Leung Ping-kwan, in: interview with scholar and translator Gordon T. Osing in Appendix 1, *City At the End of Time: Poems by Leung Ping-kwan*, edited and introduced by Esther M.K. Cheung, translated by Gordon T. Osing and Leung Ping-kwan, Hong Kong University Press, 2006 / 2012.

IV

George Denis Patrick Carlin (1937–2008)

American stand-up comedian, actor, social commentator. See his classic routine on stuff: https://www.youtube.com/watch?v=MvgN5gCuLac

Shouldering patriarchal practices

On 16 January 2016, Ms Tsai Ing-wen of the Democratic Progressive Party was elected president of Taiwan, having secured 56 per cent of the vote, defeating her two male opponents for the position. HK both cheered and jeered, this conflict of emotions being typical of his nature.

Ms Kwan's protest at LegCo meeting, 22 February, 2016

https://www.youtube.com/watch?v=uYxYP0p1Pt0 This impassioned three-minute Cantonese speech (remixed version) by Ms Rita Kwan Ying-yi succinctly summed up the frustrations of ordinary HK citizens about the blind-and-deaf ruling class of the current government. Ms Kwan is most assuredly not a princess, although perhaps she should be crowned the people's princess. This version dubbed

in English is for non-Cantonese speakers: https://
www.hongkongfp.com/2016/02/23/video-woman-
launches-fervent-tirade-against-govt-during-legco-
meeting-wins-approval-of-netizens/

V

Home to Stay

Published by Greenfield Review Press, New York,
1990. My story 'The Fourth Copy', subtitled 'Dancing with Skeletons & Other Romances', also appears
in my collection *History's Fiction*. The nineties were
a very special time for Asian-American writers and
artists in and from New York City. In 2014, our experience was documented in the anthology *Local/Express:
Asian American Arts & Community in 90's New York*
(AALR, New York), and my contribution was another
story from the same collection, 'Manky's Tale', set in
Hong Kong during Tiananmen.

Tamas Aczel (1921–1984)

Author of several novels in Hungarian and English,
and winner of the 1994 Kossuth Prize and the 1952
Stalin Prize for Literature. His papers reside at the
Special Collections archive of the UMass Amherst
Libraries. He served as director of the MFA program
at that institution from 1979 to 1982, while also
continuing to teach fiction. Prior to that, he taught

Modern European Literature.
http://scua.library.umass.edu/umarmot/aczel-tamas/

VI
Ways of saying goodbye in Chinese
http://www.fluentu.com/chinese/blog/2013/08/07/
say-goodbyechinese/ Posted by 'Alan' as an avatar
squirrel on FluentU, a Mandarin Chinese language
and culture blog that uses simplified characters. My
HK bias is showing here as I will not use simplified characters when I write (or type) Chinese. The
strokes are unnatural, not part of the DNA of my
childhood spent writing traditional characters in the
correct stroke order, over and over and over again so
that even characters I cannot read are easy to reproduce in writing, for as long as my memory serves.

University roofs collapsing
The tragic incident garnered widespread media coverage locally and elsewhere, including this piece credit-
ed to three Chinese-sounding bylines (which does not
necessarily mean the ones who sport these monikers
are, in fact, Chinese) http://www.scmp.com/news/
hong-kong/education-community/ article/1949955/
malpractice-could-have-played-role-city. Surprisingly,
the subhead uses 'rooves', an archaic plural of roof. It
appears that a linguistic memory lingers in the leading

English-language newspaper of the city, which is now owned by Alibaba's founder Jack Ma, a former English teacher who perhaps favours peculiar plurals. Also: http://www.scmp.com/news/hong-kong/article/1958842/wall-and-roof-collapse-historic-former-central-police-station-raises

Political Hopes

For a less literal and more meaningful view of what the people of the city really yearn for, see Keane Shum's piece 'The Zhang Dejiang Speech Hong Kong Hoped to Hear' http://www.scmp.com/comment/insight-opinion/article/1956380/zhang-dejiang-speech-hong-kong-had-hoped-hear a creative nonfiction experiment in speech writing that only a creative writer could pen. [Full disclosure: Keane is a MFA graduate from that same university I used to work for, the one that closed down the program].

Stealer's Wheel, 'Stuck in the Middle'

https://www.youtube.com/watch?v=DohRa9lsx0Q

'Off Season with Snake'

Which appeared in the journal *Your Impossible Voice* I reflected on this moment of my mother's Alzheimer's in my essay 'Off Season with Snake', which appeared in the Issue 7, Spring 2015 journal *Your*

Impossible Voice http://www.yourimpossiblevoice.com/off-season-with-snake/. Impossible? Yes, but the voice will out somehow, because what I do know and continue to know about myself is that I am a writer and a writer, when confronted by impossible life, writes.

The Inaugural Hong Kong Series

Hong Kong has many faces: international financial hub, home of martial arts films and cantopop, intercultural melting pot, former Crown colony and now Special Administrative Region of the People's Republic of China. When the United Kingdom transferred sovereignty over Hong Kong to China on 1 July 1997, the event not only ended 156 years of British rule, it also opened a new chapter of cultural, linguistic and political exploration. Twenty years later, Penguin Random House launches the Hong Kong Specials series. Seven outstanding literary and intellectual voices from Hong Kong take stock of the city as it is today, a city that has undergone an era of unforeseeable transition and at the same time is in the midst of forging a new identity.

Read more from these authors in the series:

Xu Xi
Antony Dapiran
Dung Kai-cheung
Simon Cartledge
Ben Bland
Christopher DeWolf
Magnus Renfrew